WITHDRAWN

General Editors: J. R. MULRYNE
and J. C. BULMAN
Associate Editor: Margaret Shewring

Cymbeline

Already published in the series

J. L. Styan *All's Well that Ends Well*
Jill Levenson *Romeo and Juliet*
Graham Holderness *The Taming of the Shrew*

In production

Hugh Richmond *Richard III*
Alan Dessen *Titus Andronicus*
J. R. Mulryne *Antony and Cleopatra*
J. C. Bulman *The Merchant of Venice*
Margaret Shewring *Richard II*
Alexander Leggatt *King Lear*
Carol Rutter *Henry VI*
Roger Savage *The Tempest*
Miriam Gilbert *Love's Labour's Lost*

Volumes on most other plays in preparation

Of related interest

J. L. Halio *Understanding Shakespeare's plays in performance*

Cymbeline

ROGER WARREN

Manchester
University Press

Manchester and New York

Distributed exclusively in the USA and Canada by St. Martin's Press

© ROGER WARREN 1989

Published by
Manchester University Press

Oxford Road, Manchester, M13 9PL
and Room 400, 175 Fifth Avenue,
New York, NY 10010, USA

*Distributed exclusively in the USA and Canada
by* St. Martin's Press, Room 400, 175 Fifth Avenue,
New York, NY 10010, USA

British Library cataloguing in publication data
Warren, Roger, *1943–*
Cymbeline – (Shakespeare in performance).
1. Drama in English. Shakespeare, William, 1564-1616
Cymbeline. Performance
I. Title II. Series
792.9'5

Library of Congress cataloging in publication data
Warren, Roger.
Cymbeline.
(Shakespeare in performance)
Bibliography: p.
Includes index.
1. Shakespeare, William, 1564-1616. Cymbeline.
2. Shakespeare, William, 1564-1616—Stage history.
I. Shakespeare, William, 1564-1616. Cymbeline.
II. Title. III. Series.
PR2806.W37   1989   822.3'3   88-27376

ISBN 0 7190 2717 9 *hardback*

Typeset by
Koinonia Limited, Manchester
Printed in Great Britain

CONTENTS

The illustrations appear between chapters V and VI (pp. 98-9)

SERIES EDITORS' PREFACE

The study of Shakespeare's plays as scripts for performance in the theatre has grown in recent years to become a major interest for many university, college and secondary-school students and their teachers. The aim of the present series is to assist this study by describing how certain of Shakespeare's texts have been realised in production.

The series is not concerned to provide theatre histories. Rather, each contributor has selected a small number of productions of a particular play and studied them comparatively. The productions, often from different periods, countries and media, have been chosen because they are significant interpretations in their own right, but also because they represent something of the range and variety of possible interpretations of the play in hand. We hope that students and theatregoers, by reading these accounts of Shakespeare in performance, may enlarge their understanding of the text and begin, too, to appreciate some of the ways in which practical considerations influence the meanings a production incorporates: the stage the actor plays on, the acting company, the player's own physique and abilities, stage-design and theatre-tradition, as well as the political, social and economic conditions of performance and the expectations of a particular audience.

Any study of a Shakespeare text will reveal only a small proportion of the text's potential meaning. We hope that the effect of this series will be to encourage a kind of reading that is receptive to the ever-varying discoveries theatre interpretation provides.

J. R. Mulryne
J. C. Bulman
Margaret Shewring

PREFATORY NOTE

My greatest debt is to the actors, directors, and designers whose work is described here. My first experience of *Cymbeline* in performance was at Stratford-upon-Avon in 1957. That production was recorded by BBC radio, and re-broadcast some ten years later, enabling me to check my initial impressions, especially on points of detail. For the 1970 version at Stratford, Ontario, I have had to rely on the theatre's videotape of the production. I have naturally drawn upon reviews or prompt-books for documentary evidence, but I have not admitted any material about performances which I have not been able to verify for myself, apart from the brief stage history at the end of chapter I. My thanks to the archives and press offices of the theatres concerned for their help.

A draft typescript was read by both general editors, and by J. S. Cunningham, Judith Dunbar, and Stanley Wells. I have greatly benefited from their friendly encouragement, and from their detailed suggestions. My visits to Stratford, Ontario, were made possible by research awards from the British Academy, and I am very grateful for their support.

RW
1988

NOTE ON THE TEXT

All quotations from Shakespeare are from Stanley Wells and Gary Taylor, general editors, *William Shakespeare, The Complete Works* (Oxford, 1986). Their text of *Cymbeline* contains two major departures from more familiar versions which call for comment. The Oxford Shakespeare represents the most rigorous and logical modernisation of Shakespeare so far, and this includes replacing the Elizabethan spelling of proper names by their modern equivalents. So the First Folio's spelling 'Iachimo' is replaced by the modern form of the name, 'Giacomo'. But by far the most radical departure from tradition is that the heroine is not called 'Imogen', as in the Folio, but 'Innogen'.

Editors have long suspected that the form 'Imogen', unknown before *Cymbeline*, is not a Shakespearian coinage but a misprint for 'Innogen', because in Simon Forman's manuscript account of a contemporary performance, the heroine's name is quite clearly 'Innogen'. (The document is reproduced in S. Schoenbaum, *William Shakespeare: A Documentary Life*, 1975, p. 215.) This makes it virtually certain that this was the name that Shakespeare gave her, and it is supported by other evidence. In Holinshed's *Chronicles*, upon which Shakespeare drew for his Ancient British material, the legendary first queen of Britain is called 'Innogen', so this would have seemed an apt name for a mythical British princess. Besides, 'Innogen', with its overtones of innocence, gives the character a significant name like those of other heroines in Shakespeare's late plays – Marina, 'born at sea', in *Pericles*; Perdita, 'lost for ever', in *The Winter's Tale*; Miranda, 'the top of admiration', in *The Tempest* – and in *Cymbeline* itself it matches the symbolic name that the character assumes as a page: 'Fidele', the faithful one. And Shakespeare had used 'Innogen' before: in the opening stage direction of *Much Ado About Nothing*, he introduces 'Leonato' and 'Innogen his wife'. He subsequently dropped the character of the wife from the play, but the fact that he had called a husband and wife Leonato and Innogen prior to *Cymbeline* makes it natural that he should have linked the two names again for Posthumus Leonatus and Innogen.

All this evidence fully justifies the Oxford reading; and for the sake of consistency throughout the book, I have used the forms 'Giacomo' and 'Innogen' even in quotations from other writers who have used the Folio's 'Iachimo' and 'Imogen'.

CHAPTER I

Theatrical issues

Theatrical virtuosity

The most striking theatrical quality of *Cymbeline* is its capacity to astonish and to move an audience at the same time. Its impact in performance depends upon combining strokes of theatrical virtuosity with language of exceptional evocative power. At the heart of the play are three extraordinary scenes: Giacomo emerging from a trunk in the midnight quiet of Innogen's bedroom; the funeral rites ceremonially spoken over Innogen's body, followed by her revival beside Cloten's headless corpse dressed in her husband's clothes; and the descent of Jupiter on an eagle's back to Posthumus in prison. Bemused commentators have sought to account for such apparently bizarre events in terms of tragedy 'petering out', or tragi-comedy, or romance, or self-conscious 'coterie dramaturgy' specifically designed for court performance. *Cymbeline* contains all these elements, and different stagings have emphasised different aspects; but as a whole it resists conventional labels. A play of such overt theatricality demands to be considered in theatrical terms; and an account of the play as experienced in performance helps to explain why it is written as it is.

Startling events communicated by virtuoso theatrical means are features that *Cymbeline* shares with two other plays, *The Winter's Tale* and *The Tempest*, that Shakespeare wrote at roughly the same time (1610-11), with *Pericles* (1607-08) in some respects a forerunner. The jealousy that strikes Leontes like a bolt from the blue and the coming to life of Hermione's statue in *The Winter's Tale*, or Prospero's magic in *The Tempest*, executed as a series of theatrical shows, have much in common with the theatricality of *Cymbeline*. In 1608, Shakespeare's theatre company, the King's Men, acquired an indoor playhouse, the Blackfriars, smaller and more intimate than their outdoor theatre, the Globe, and it has been argued that this move encouraged Shakespeare to these experiments in theatrical virtuosity. It has also been suggested that the elaborate spectacle, especially the descent of Jupiter, was inspired by court masques of the period, some of them designed by Inigo Jones, who later provided a design for Jupiter on an eagle in Townshend's masque *Tempe Restored* of 1632. Yet the King's Men continued to play at the Globe. On 15 May 1611, the schoolmaster and astrologer Simon Forman saw *The Winter's Tale* at the Globe; and some time before 8 September 1611, when he died, he also saw *Cymbeline*; unfortunately he does not say where and when, but it is likely to have been in the same theatre, where he could have seen it more cheaply than at the Blackfriars, at roughly the same time. Certainly, while *Cymbeline* does have intimate scenes, it also has very large-scale ones, like the battle and the descent of Jupiter, and modern performances have usually been given on large stages like the Royal Shakespeare Theatre at Stratford-upon-Avon or the vast open stage at Stratford, Ontario, where the play's large-scale theatricality has room to open out. It seems, by contrast, very cramped on television and, at least in some scenes, in a studio like The Other Place at Stratford-upon-Avon.

Myth and pseudo-history

Whether given at Blackfriars or at the Globe, on huge stages or small ones, *Cymbeline* creates its own self-sufficient world. Shakespeare draws upon widely disparate stories from folk-tale and from pseudo-history for the mythical realm of Cymbeline's Britain. The wager upon Innogen's chastity derives primarily from Boccaccio's *Decameron* and from a German version of the story known in an English translation as *Frederick of Jennen*. But the other two main plots, the stories of the kidnapped princes and the framing narrative about the war between Britain and Rome, come from widely separated sections of Holinshed's *Chronicles of England and Scot-*

land. An obvious challenge for the director and designer is the range of reference that results: Boccaccio's medieval-to-Renaissance Italy, represented in the play by Giacomo, is a world of intrigue very different from the classical Rome ruled by Augustus Caesar and represented by Caius Lucius. In his 1957 production at Stratford-upon-Avon, Peter Hall took the bull by the horns and boldly emphasised this range through a deliberate clash of costume: Roman togas jostled with medieval doublets, druids with Renaissance courtiers. On the same stage in 1962, William Gaskill presented a basically medieval world: Innogen was a medieval princess, but for her male disguise she changed into a rough homespun garment that suggested an earlier, more primitive era, and her brothers wore animal furs. Other productions have opted for shapeless, 'timeless' garments; but after a very unsuccessful production in would-be timeless costume at Stratford-upon-Avon in 1979, Robert Cushman wondered whether the play might not work better in Jacobean dress than in the 'legendary-nondescript get-up affected here' (*Observer*, 22 April 1979).

This suggestion usefully raises a further complicating factor when attempting to establish a coherent theatrical world for *Cymbeline*, its contemporary element. In 1961 Emrys Jones asked what impression it might have made upon its original audiences: 'Why did Shakespeare choose that particular king? What interest would King Cymbeline have had for Shakespeare's audiences?' ('Stuart *Cymbeline*', reprinted in D. J. Palmer, ed., *Shakespeare's Later Comedies*, 1971, p. 251). The only conceivable reason for Shakespeare's choice of Cymbeline rather than any other remote king from the pages of Holinshed was that he was supposed to have ruled Britain when Christ was born. He was a prince of peace at a time of universal peace, and this may have been designed to appeal to King James I, who liked to see himself as the peace-maker of Europe. If so, it would help to explain why the title role of this play is so slightly characterised: he is important not as a character but as a figure-head. At the end he is what Emrys Jones calls him, 'simply the great Western King ... magnanimously radiating Peace'. Jones adds that not only the character but the whole play suffer 'from being too close to its royal audience' (p. 261).

This royal link may have been an important part of the play's impact for its original audience; is it possible to convey any of this to a modern one? John Barton attempted to do so in 1974 at Stratford-upon-Avon. He presented *Cymbeline* in the context of *Richard*

II and *King John*. All three plays were given in the same curtained, chamber setting, with the cast dressed basically in sober brown Jacobean doublets and boots, to which they added accessories as relevant. So Richard II, Bolingbroke when he became king, and King John all wore the same glittering gold robe as the symbol of their royalty, and Cymbeline assumed this robe as 'the great Western King' at the end of his play. But Frank Kermode, reviewing the production in *The Times Literary Suplement* of 5 July 1974, could not persuade himself that this presentation of Cymbeline as a symbolic figure 'made much difference'. That was partly because this flimsy role will take no interpretative straining at it, and partly because Jacobean dress has no significant resonances for modern audiences. Robin Phillips had originally intended to use Jacobean costume for his production at Stratford, Ontario, in 1986 specifically to bring out the connection with James I; but in the event he came to feel that a form of modern dress would best recreate the experience of Jacobean audiences, and he finally set the production in the late 1930s and early 1940s since this provided recognisable images both of royal figures and of a world war. Practical experience so far suggests that the link with James I is of historical interest only, with no discernible advantages for the play in modern performance.

Ovidian technique

While Boccaccio and Holinshed are the main sources as far as plot is concerned, another writer was arguably a still more important influence upon the dramatic technique of the play. When Giacomo has stolen Innogen's bracelet, and is about to return to the trunk, he notes a book beside the bed:

> She hath been reading late,
> The tale of Tereus. Here the leaf's turned down
> Where Philomel gave up. (II.ii.44-6)

This allusion contributes to the atmosphere of potential rape in the scene: Tereus raped his sister-in-law Philomel and tore out her tongue; in revenge, she and her sister Procne served Tereus with a cannibal meal consisting of the flesh of his young son. As he pursued them in frenzy, all three of them were turned into birds.

[4]

The story is told in Ovid's *Metamorphoses*, one of Shakespeare's favourite books, to judge from the number of times he draws upon it in his work. He alludes to the Philomel story, for instance, throughout *Titus Andronicus*, to intensify a parallel story of rape, mutilation, and cannibal revenge, and even brings Ovid's book itself on to the stage. Though Shakespeare does not specify the book that Innogen is reading, we may reasonably deduce that it too is the *Metamorphoses*. The connections between *Cymbeline* and the *Metamorphoses*, however, occur not so much in the events, apart perhaps from Cloten's plan to rape Innogen and mutilate Posthumus only to end up mutilated himself, as in the general technique.

In an important article, 'The Metamorphosis of Violence in *Titus Andronicus*', (*Shakespeare Survey 10*, 1957), Eugene Waith shows how both Ovid and Shakespeare are 'interested in the transforming power of intense states of emotion' (p. 41) – to the point, in Ovid, of actual transformation into animals, birds, trees, or flowers. Waith's description of Ovid's characters at the moment of their transformation, 'caught in some fantastic pose in the midst of their most violent actions' (p. 39), also fits Innogen's scene by Cloten's corpse perfectly, and 'fantastic pose' would be a very good description of Giacomo emerging from the trunk or Jupiter poised on his eagle in mid-air. At such moments, wonder and astonishment are combined with violence and intensity. At the climax of the Tereus/Philomel story that Innogen was reading about, at the very moment of their transformation into birds, Ovid has a kind of verbal double-take: 'You would have thought they were on wings; they *were* on wings!' 'We are left', says Waith, 'with these moments of wonder, caught in a series of vivid pictures' (p. 43), an apt description too of the trunk, burial, and Jupiter scenes; and Waith's phrase 'horrible and pathetic, but above all extraordinary' (p. 48) applies absolutely to the theatrical effect of Innogen's scene by the headless body.

But Ovid's *Metamorphoses* is relevant in another way. The book was a favourite with Shakespeare, I think, because it shows human beings closely related to – actually turned into – aspects of the natural world. Waith points out that in Ovid's presentation of the characters it is as if 'sheer intensity of feeling made them indistinguishable from other forms of life' (p. 42). In *Cymbeline*, Shakespeare carries to an extreme a technique that he frequently uses throughout his work: he draws upon comparisons to the natural

[5]

world in order to express 'intensity of feeling', for example when Innogen expresses the sharpness of her pain by asking the gods merely for 'as small a drop of pity / As a wren's eye' (IV.ii. 306-7). But Shakespeare takes this technique much further in Arviragus's flower-speech over the apparently dead Innogen, a speech that goes well beyond superficial compliment. It identifies Innogen with various aspects of the natural world until by the end of the speech she has almost become a part of that world, covered by 'furred moss':

> With fairest flowers,
> Whilst summer lasts and I live here, Fidele,
> I'll sweeten thy sad grave. Thou shalt not lack
> The flower that's like thy face, pale primrose, nor
> The azured harebell, like thy veins; no, nor
> The leaf of eglantine, whom not to slander
> Outsweetened not thy breath. The ruddock would
> With charitable bill – O bill sore shaming
> Those rich-left heirs that let their fathers lie
> Without a monument! – bring thee all this,
> Yea, and furred moss besides, when flowers are none,
> To winter-gown thy corpse. (IV.ii.219-30)

The remarkable language here, and in the famous dirge 'Fear no more the heat o' th' sun' that follows, seems to strike a chord in most audiences, to judge from the tense, hushed stillness that usually prevails in the theatre at this point. The still beauty and gravity of the language presumably appeals to deep-rooted human instincts, communicating a sense of profound loss and of tender love for the person celebrated; and it does so by evoking a world of primal simplicity that is explicitly contrasted with the hypocrisy of much human mourning: the robin's charity is set against human heirs 'that let their fathers lie / Without a monument'. It is a characteristic of the technique of *Cymbeline* that this crucial point is made in a parenthesis; when directors cut such lines, as they often do because omitting parentheses is a convenient way of shortening speeches, they rob the text of its richness and power of implication. But audiences, when they are allowed to, respond to such implications; that is how the scene works. The power of the language makes them share in the princes' grief and love for Innogen, and also in the strange consolation of the speech as Innogen becomes part of the natural world – just as, in the midst of the barbarity of Ovid's tale of Philomel, there is a consolatory note: as if in compensation for losing her tongue, she is turned into the nightingale, the bird that is celebrated for the melodious beauty of its song. A similar mixture of beauty and barbarity is very much part of our experience of this sequence in *Cymbeline*, where the simple pathos of this speech and of the dirge is set against the savage spectacle of Cloten's headless corpse. Innogen herself summarises this mixture of extremes when she wakes:

> These flowers are like the pleasures of the world,
> This bloody man the care on't. (IV.ii.298-9)

For all its potency, however, the language does not work in isolation. A distinctive quality of the play in performance is that it combines such language with the theatrical virtuosity in order to isolate, almost to spotlight, individual human emotions on stage in extreme form: love, despair, jealousy, even death and burial, ultimately reconciliation. In his book *Shakespeare in the Theatre* (1978), Richard David describes 'the shattering effect of the simplicities that suddenly shine out from its complexities and obscurities', like the dirge and 'such lines as Arviragus' "The bird is dead / That we have made so much on", as he carries out the apparently dead Fidele from the cave' (p. 188). The impact of this moment in performance is frequently commented upon by reviewers. The moment itself is, as David says, 'shattering' in its simplicity; but it is important to note that those very 'complexities and obscurities' have helped to create it. The First Folio's stage direction catches its force: 'Enter Arviragus with Innogen, dead, bearing her in his arms.' Editors sometimes emend 'dead' to 'as dead', since the audience knows that Innogen has taken a drug, not poison, because the doctor Cornelius told them so in I.v: but at this moment, by theatrical sleight of hand, Shakespeare has it both ways; he creates a magical moment in which that knowledge is not so much forgotten as suppressed. The audience responds to the pathos of the moment, and particularly to the poignant simplicity of Arviragus's words.

Complicating fairy-tale characters

An important dramatic function of the language is to complicate the stereotypes to which the characters appear to conform. At first, they seem to have the simplicity of fairy-tale: innocent heroine, wronged hero, villain, grotesque simpleton, and so on. But the density of the language they speak modifies this initial impression. Giacomo's soliloquy in Innogen's bedroom complicates the image of an Italianate intriguer, just as the sheer emotional range of Innogen's language makes her more than a fairy-tale princess. Posthumus and Cloten appear to be opposites, the one a *chevalier sans peur et sans reproche* (a fearless and irreproachable knight), the other a 'clotpoll'. But a disconcerting consequence of the language is to suggest similarities as well as contrasts between them. When Posthumus thinks that Innogen has betrayed him, he exclaims:

> O that I had her here to tear her limb-meal!
> I will go there and do't i' th' court, before
> Her father. (II.iv.147-9)

His violent threats to Innogen here are very close to those of Cloten:

> When my lust hath dined – which, as I say, to vex her I will execute in the clothes that she so praised – to the court I'll knock her back, foot her home again. (III.v.141-4)

This connection suggests one reason why Shakespeare contrives the situation where Innogen wakes beside Cloten's body dressed in Posthumus's clothes, and why he compels her to make so positive an identification of the body: the physical similarity hints at a psychological similarity – within, of course, a basic contrast of personality. Usually actors of the two parts go exclusively for the contrast; but there is a case for stressing the similarities in performance, and even for doubling the roles, though I have only seen this done once, at the Royal Exchange Theatre, Manchester, in 1984. Such doubling would normally require slight textual re-arrangements, since for example Cloten's exit at the end of II.iii is immediately followed by Posthumus's entry at the start of II.iv; but here, since the costumes were extremely rudimentary, the actor merely had to put on or discard differentiating accessories. Unfortunately the unimaginative monotony of the costumes extended to the whole production, so that virtually no inter-pretative discoveries could be made. The practical results of this double, therefore, remain to be investigated.

Elijah Moshinsky, director of the BBC television version, claims that Shakespeare has complicated the characters to the point where each has 'several identities: Innogen becomes Fidele, . . .

the Queen is duplicitous of her nature, Cloten dresses up as Post-humus' (BBC edition, 1983, p. 18). This allows each character to be interpreted very variously, particularly the Queen. Claire Bloom, who plays the part in Moshinsky's production, calls her a 'splintered character' (BBC edition, p. 22). The Queen has so many different 'faces' – fairy-tale witch, wicked stepmother, patriotic defier of the Romans, queen mother – that no modern performance of the part has been really comparable with another. Joan Miller (Stratford-upon-Avon, 1957) was a sinister black-clad stepmother from a Grimm fairy-tale; Sheila Allen (Stratford, 1974) was a glamorous sorceress in a silk robe decorated with all the colours of the rainbow, a radiant beauty who fully explained Cymbeline's besotted obsession with her; and Claire Bloom herself was a Medici Queen Mother, never more smilingly condescending than when planning to poison her victims: she gave her threat to poison Inno-gen, which Joan Miller delivered between clenched teeth, a thoughtful tone of sweet reasonableness:

> and which she after,
> Except she bend her humour, shall be assured
> To taste of too. (I.v.80-2)

Thus easily, it was implied, did the Medicis dispose of their oppon-ents. Perhaps a role that permits distinguished actresses to give such strikingly differentiated performances should make us hesi-tate before agreeing too readily with Robert Speaight that this is 'arguably the worst part that Shakespeare ever wrote' (*Shakespeare on the Stage*, 1973, p. 252).

Modern performance demonstrates something different about Belarius and the two stolen princes. Interpretation of these roles does not vary greatly from production to production; their scenes are almost unfailingly effective. And here, theatrical experience places in perspective the claims of scholarly commentators, begin-ning with Dr Johnson in his edition of Shakespeare (1765). Belarius's soliloquy (III.iii.79-107), which tells the audience that his 'sons' are actually the princes and how he abducted them and brought them up, provoked Johnson to observe tartly: 'this sol-iloquy is very inartificial, there being no particular reason why Belarius should now tell to himself what he could not know better by telling it'. Some modern critics explain this as an example of Shakespeare advertising the fact that this is 'only a play': in this interpretation, Belarius must be taken simply as a cardboard story-book figure. But in performance the supposed awkwardness ('inartificiality') of the speech disappears. In the BBC television production, for example, Michael Gough effortlessly communicates the warmth and integrity of the character, not by distracting from the lines with some ingeniously slanted interpretation, but by speaking them simply and directly. Nor is he an isolated case. Writing of William Gaskill's 1962 production, the anonymous reviewer in *The Times* thought that the 'most beautiful thing of all in the play seemed to be the relationship between the exiled Belarius and the two stolen princes' (18 July 1962).

This is a large and significant claim to make about a section of the play which has drawn critical derision from others beside Johnson. According to J. M. Nosworthy, editor of the new Arden edition (1955), the princes are merely symbolic figures who are 'an embarrassment to actor, producer and audience' (p. lii). To this J. C. Maxwell retorted, in his New Shakespeare edition (1960): 'I find a good deal of stage vitality in the princes, and in all the productions I have seen, the nonchalance of Guiderius's "I cut off's head" (V.vi.297) has roused genuine (and unembarrassed) laughter' (p. xxxviii). All the performances I have seen, too, bear Maxwell out. And he raises another consequential theatrical issue when he says that 'it is not possible to describe [the wager plot] as "central" with absolute confidence' (p. xxxviii). The wager plot starts things off, and Giacomo's contribution, in particular, is crucial; without an adequate Giacomo the play simply cannot work at all, as the 1979 production at Stratford-upon-Avon demonstrated the hard way. But once the Giacomo/Posthumus plot has got the play going, the momentum is then sustained by the Belarius/princes plot, with Innogen as the character who moves between the two plots and holds them together.

In *Shakespeare Survey 16* (1963), John Russell Brown observed how the reunion of Innogen and her brothers in William Gaskill's 1962 version 'held the audience by its large impression of new-born wonder and spontaneous joy' (p. 150). Peter Thomson, reviewing the following Stratford production (1974), made the same point about this moment, adding: 'This is an almost unfailingly effective stage event, with far more impact than could be easily predicted from a reading' (*Shakespeare Survey 28*, 1975, p. 143). Part of the impact of this moment derives, of course, from the fact that Shakespeare sets up their mutual affection (and the princes' sense of loss in the burial scene) so affectingly earlier on. And since he establishes an equally convincing relationship betwen Belarius and his foster-sons, their parting at the end is very moving, especially Belarius's farewell blessing:

> The benediction of these covering heavens
> Fall on their heads like dew, for they are worthy
> To inlay heaven with stars. (V.vi.352-4)

Cymbeline's following line ('Thou weep'st, and speak'st') indicates how Belarius delivers his lines, choked with emotion, and that has often been the response of the audience: John Russell Brown found Paul Hardwick's delivery of the blessing in 1962 'affecting by clear and large transitions of mood', and the sight of the two princes clinging to the weeping Michael Gough, refusing to be parted from him, is perhaps the most moving moment of the BBC television version. The emotional power of these scenes comes primarily from the simple but highly-charged phrases, and actors naturally make the most of them. As Russell Brown says, some moments in the play 'need a simple, unreflecting strength'. Not all of *Cymbeline* consists of complexity and theatrical virtuosity; a review of Bill Alexander's 1987 production at The Other Place in Stratford-upon-Avon pointed out that though the play is 'ornate and . . . elaborate, it is also one of the simplest and most heartfelt romances he wrote' (Andrew Rissek, *The Independent*, 14 November 1987).

'Tragedy petering out'

The First Folio calls the play a tragedy; but as E. M. W. Tillyard remarks in his book *Shakespeare's Last Plays* (1938), 'the tragic events . . . are curiously apt to end in insignificance'; and he analyses Posthumus's soliloquy (II.v) as an example of what he calls 'tragedy petering out' (pp. 27-9). After Giacomo's apparent proof that Innogen is disloyal, Tillyard argues, we naturally expect a tragic response. The speech begins with tragic intensity but ends with 'a conventional cynicism like that of Donne's satires' as Posthumus merely declares that he will *write* against women, and concludes, more cynically still:

> yet 'tis greater skill
> In a true hate to pray they have their will. (II.v.33-4)

That couplet sounds as if it is the conclusion of the speech; but then Posthumus adds a parting shot, almost as an afterthought: 'The very devils cannot plague them better.' Tillyard rightly concludes that this ending is 'quite remote from tragic feeling'. The mistake is to argue, as he does, that this is a fault, as if Shakespeare were attempting to write tragedy, but not being tragic enough. The careful modulations of tone in the soliloquy, especially that single line which concludes it and defuses the finality of the couplet, make it plain that Shakespeare is deliberately steering the character away from tragedy.

The sense of Shakespeare raising tragic expectations only to provide something surprisingly different recurs in the bedroom scene, where Giacomo does not attempt to seduce Innogen – Granville-Barker says in his *Preface* to the play that 'no tragically-potent scoundrel . . . will ever come out of a trunk' (1930, reprinted 1984, p. 58) – and still more when Innogen awakes by the headless body she takes to be her husband's: her impassioned expressions of grief and pain might lead the audience to expect the speech to resolve tragically, with her suicide; but instead, she agrees to serve Caius Lucius as his page, and so paves the way for the happy ending. The whole thrust of the play, and especially of this scene, is ultimately away from tragedy. Shakespeare seems to be developing a dramatic technique which manipulates events so that characters are placed in situations where they confront the possibility of tragedy, and sometimes express emotions with the intensity of tragedy, without actually having to endure a tragic outcome.

This placing of potentially tragic situations within a context of elaborate theatricality which ultimately frustrates tragic expectation has led influential modern critics like A. C. Kirsch and R. A. Foakes to argue that the play's 'theatrical self-consciousness' is deliberately designed to keep reminding the audience of the artificiality of the play, so as to distance them from the events on stage, and especially to prevent them from becoming too involved with the emotions of the characters in the way that a fully tragic technique might have invited. One of the most important questions this book tries to answer is whether theatrical experience bears out this contention. It is one of many issues raised in extreme form by those three overtly theatrical central scenes I mentioned at the start – the trunk, burial, and Jupiter scenes – and it is worth considering their theatrical potential in some detail.

Self-conscious artifice or basic humanity?

When Giacomo emerges from the trunk in Innogen's bedroom the way that the scene works is that the slow lifting of the lid and the stealthy emergence of Giacomo, so close to the sleeping Innogen, acts as a kind of sensational 'call to attention', screwing up the tension in order to throw particular emphasis on what Giacomo is to do and to say. In view of the terms of the wager, we expect a rape scene, and this expectation is reinforced by Giacomo's reference to Tarquin's rape of Lucrece in his opening lines:

> Our Tarquin thus
> Did softly press the rushes ere he wakened
> The chastity he wounded. (II.ii.12-14)

Expectation is utterly confounded: he does not even attempt to rape her, but delivers instead a lyrical tribute to her beauty and worth, the most exquisite moment of which is this detail:

> On her left breast
> A mole, cinque-spotted, like the crimson drops
> I' th' bottom of a cowslip. (II.ii.37-9)

But of course Giacomo will turn this detail to sinister use, persuading Posthumus that he has won the wager; and the overtones of rape return at the end of the speech, as Giacomo notices that she has been reading about Tereus's rape of Philomel. Although Giacomo does not actually rape Innogen, the threat coexists, in the tense atmosphere of the scene, with the lyrical beauty of Giacomo's tribute to Innogen; it is a dangerous invasion of her privacy. That is certainly how Elijah Moshinsky takes it in his BBC television production: 'The removal of the bracelet is in fact a rape' (BBC edition, p. 23). And some recent productions have emphasised Giacomo's intimacy with Innogen by having him straddle her; and even pull the bedclothes completely away from her. In such circumstances, she may not actually be raped, but she is certainly defiled by his attentions. Such stagings stress the darker implications of the speech; others have taken the scene much more lightly and have emphasised instead the lyricism and elegance, even a vein of ironic humour. Here, Giacomo becomes a sophisticated voyeur rather than a potential rapist.

Light or dark, these interpretations are suggested by different aspects of the speech itself. They assume, in short, that the point of the theatrical business with the trunk is to focus attention on the speech and what it is about, not that the use of the trunk is a device to send up the whole situation with, as it were, a knowing wink to the audience. But that is how it was played by Ian Richardson at Stratford-upon-Avon and subsequently in London in 1974, within the context of a production by John Barton which emphasised and exaggerated the artifice and 'theatrical self-consciousness' of the whole play by extending the ironic framework which some critics believe Shakespeare has provided for it. His main device was to enlarge the role of the doctor Cornelius to a kind of 'presenter' like Gower in *Pericles*. Cornelius spoke the lines of the first gentleman at the start (as in Gaskill's and Moshinsky's productions) and of the Roman Soothsayer (as in Hall's). Cornelius also 'framed' several scenes, particularly the battle, by speaking stage directions from the First Folio and passages from Holinshed. But it was not so much the alterations themselves as the facetious tone in which they were delivered that provided the ironic frame. Irving Wardle described the effect: Cornelius

> sets the tone of the occasion as a fairy-tale in which anything can happen, take it or leave it. 'The scene changeth to Italy', he remarks with a helpless shrug; and in the hysterical final pile-up of reunions and long-lost moles on the neck, he brings the house down with a panicky: 'O gods! / I left out one thing.' You are, in short, encouraged to laugh at the play. (*The Times*, 21 December 1974)

In this mocking context, Ian Richardson gave a characteristically over-the-top account of the bedroom scene, as Frank Kermode pointed out disapprovingly in *The Times Literary Supplement*: 'In her chamber he popped up like Punch out of the trunk, . . . all banter and jokey Gielgudian tremolo, with more giggles in the audience' (5 July 1974). Giacomo's soliloquy condenses the passing of three hours into five minutes or so. Most productions mark this speeding-up of normal time into stage time by the periodic striking of a clock during the speech. Peter Hall in 1957, for instance, had midnight strike before Giacomo emerged, one o'clock thirteen lines later, just before 'But my design – / To note the chamber' (II.ii.23-4), two o' clock only seven lines after that, just before 'O sleep, thou ape of death' (l.31), and three o' clock at the end of the speech, as the Folio instructs: *'Clock strikes'*. Giacomo listens, and counts the chimes: 'One, two, three'. The whole process is a kind of theatrical shorthand which, as in countless other examples in drama, an audience simply accepts as such without a second thought, unless positively invited to notice it. Barton and Richardson did invite them to notice it, by having the clock strike two and then three as if the hours were speeding by in quick succession: 'One – two? – three?!?' cried Richardson in startled amazement, with double-takes, getting gales of laughter, before popping back into his trunk. There could be no suggestion of stillness, tension, or danger in such a rendering.

Frank Kermode rightly censured this trivialising of a subtle speech; but, nervously aware that his adverse criticism of the approach was coming dangerously close to invalidating the critical view that Shakespeare is playing with the play, distancing us from it, making us laugh at it, he tried to avoid the logical implications of this production for critical argument: 'Well, we are told that this is a play that constantly draws attention to its own theatrical-ity; but this is not the same thing as advising the audience that there's nothing they need feel uneasy about.' This face-saving dis-tinction is sophistical: Richardson's performance demonstrated precisely what theories about Shakespeare playing with the play amount to in practice.

The question arises still more acutely in Innogen's scene beside Cloten's headless body. This is the central scene of the play; it is also, in my experience, the scene with the greatest impact in per-formance: there is the sense, as you get to it, that this is the heart of the matter. This is, so to speak, what Shakespeare wrote the play for. But how are we to take it? Why has Shakespeare manipu-lated events so as to present us with ceremonial burial rites for someone who is not in fact dead, and who makes a detailed, heartbroken but erroneous identification of a dead body? The ques-tion is bound to arise when reading, less so for an audience caught up in a performance; and the reason for that is that they are not standing back evaluating the scene, but experiencing it. So how do they react? Does the audience's knowledge that the headless corpse is in fact Cloten's distance them from Innogen's grief? Do they, as influential criticism argues, remain detachedly superior to her grief, or does she involve them in her situation?

Once again, as in the bedroom scene, there is the question of laughter. A review of Peter Hall's 1957 production complained that it 'could not prevent that deadly laughter breaking in most fatally upon her outburst of grief over the headless body' (*Leamington Spa Courier*, 5 July 1957). We need to ask whether laughter is 'deadly', 'fatal', in this scene, and even whether an Innogen should try to prevent it. It depends to some extent on what kind of laughter it is. John Russell Brown, reviewing Vanessa Redgrave's performance in 1962, said that Cloten's headless body 'was an object which raised the nervous laughter which normally greets a too-obvious disturbance of the accepted mode of illusion in a play' but that nevertheless the audience was 'held in rapt belief and concern' by Vanessa Redgrave's performance (*Shakespeare Survey 16*, p. 150). *This* kind of nervous laughter is clearly not 'deadly' or 'fatal'. But what if the laughter is derisive, the audience laughing at the character? If, as the 'distancing' critics claim, the point of the scene is to prevent audience involvement with Innogen's plight, then mocking laughter is a very good means of achieving this. But I can state categorically that no Innogen I have seen has ever played for laughs in this scene; they have all played it 'for real', and each audience, catching the spirit of the actress's performance, has taken it so, apart from the nervous giggles that Russell Brown mentions. Such giggles are quite different from those that Ian Richardson played for in the bedroom scene, and it is worth pointing out that even in that production, which actually set the play within an ironic framework, human realities triumphed over the artifice in this scene.

Richard David represented the opinion of most reviewers in his detailed account of how Susan Fleetwood played the scene in that production and how the audience responded to it:

> Miss Fleetwood certainly succeeded with the first uneasy stirrings from Innogen's sleep in holding the theatre before the sense of the absurd could get out of hand. . . . There was true pathos in the gesturing fingers at the plea for heaven's pity, 'as small a drop . . . as a wren's eye'. What Miss Fleetwood did, in the vivid phrasing and intonation of 'The dream's here still – not imagined, FELT' . . . was to involve the audience in the nightmare quality of the experience and in its power, so that detached and critical spectatorship was impossible. (*Shakespeare in the Theatre*, p. 186)

David moves from the particular example to a general summary of the play's technique: 'the artifice, though Shakespeare resorted to it more openly and even with more self-conscious bravado than before, is used to enhance rather than to contradict the reality of the basic human situations presented. . . . Shakespeare was prepared to take hair-raising short-cuts in order to get his crucial situations onto the stage with the maximum expedition' (pp. 127, 181). The artifice focuses attention upon the human situations, expressed in exceptionally evocative language, and to those human situations the audience responds.

Shakespeare asks a very great deal from both audience and actors in this scene. It contains huge transitions, 'short-cuts' even, from the stillness, serenity, and consolation of the dirge 'Fear no more the heat o' th' sun' to the violence of Innogen's soliloquy, and from there to the poignant tenderness of her scene with Caius Lucius. The technique is extremely daring and sophisticated. First, as I suggested earlier, the language makes the audience fully experience the sadness of death and the princes' sense of loss; but the intricacies of the plot have ensured that the death is not a real one, so that the audience is next plunged into Innogen's grief as she revives, and asked to experience that also, to go through the nightmare with her. She is put through this ordeal, not as some wanton theatrical flourish, but specifically so that she can express the full range of tragic emotions – without having to suffer a tragic ending.

In her encounter with Caius Lucius, she makes a further transition from the intensity of the soliloquy to the simple pathos with which she speaks of her existence without her husband:

> I am nothing; or if not
> Nothing to be were better. (IV.ii.369-70)

It is above all her love for Posthumus that this situation enables her to express:

> There is no more such masters. I may wander
> From east to occident, cry out for service,
> Try many, all good; serve truly, never
> Find such another master. (IV.ii.373-6)

She then proposes to draw on the same natural resources to shelter the body as the princes had earlier promised to her:

> and when
> With wild-wood leaves and weeds I ha' strewed his grave
> And on it said a century of prayers,
> Such as I can, twice o'er I'll weep and sigh (IV.ii.391-4).

But exquisitely expressed as this sadness is, the crucial point of the scene, and the turning-point of the whole play, comes with Innogen's decision to turn away from grief, 'And leaving so his service, follow you'; and it is this positive decision which leads ultimately to her reunion with Posthumus. The entire technique of this play seems to push to extremes a basic principle of Shakespearian comedy: the final happiness seems the richer and more valuable for the harsh experiences that the characters have had to endure. Agnes Latham puts this well in her new Arden edition of *As You Like It* (1975), when she says that comedy 'needs something to strive against' (p. xc). Obstacles need to be placed in the path of lovers if their happy ending is not to seem facile, too easily won. Shakespeare provides both heroine and actress with formidable obstacles here.

There are obvious connections between this scene and Posthumus's vision of Jupiter. Both depend upon theatrical virtuosity, sensationalism even, but equally both are centred upon an internal, psychological crisis. It is often claimed – for example by Elijah Moshinsky in the BBC television edition – that Jupiter intervenes to change the potentially tragic course of the action; but that tragic course has already been changed by those two crucial decisions of the heroine and hero, Innogen's to go on living despite believing her husband dead, Posthumus's to forgive her *before* discovering that she was in fact innocent of adultery. The resolution in *Cymbeline* is brought about by human decisions, and the supernatural only ratifies that. In the Jupiter scene, as in others, what Richard David calls the 'basic human situation' is what counts, and the function of the startling theatricality is to focus attention upon it.

The Jupiter scene, therefore, should be considered as the climax of a series of events intended to restore Posthumus to the centre of the action after an absence of two entire acts. From his return, he is the focus of attention almost without interruption, from his soliloquy (V.i) by way of the battle (V.ii,iii) and his long account of it (V.iv) to his imprisonment and prayer, culminating in his vision of his ghostly family and of Jupiter (V.v). And even then the sequence is not ended, since after the ghosts have gone, he awakes for his soliloquy about the strangeness of it all and for his conversation with the jailer. The actor of Posthumus has a great weight of responsibility here, though this is only clear in full or fullish texts, like those used by William Gaskill, Robin Phillips, or Bill Alexander. It is surely significant that Posthumus made a greater impact in these productions than in those where much of this sequence was omitted.

John Barton, for example, replaced Posthumus's narration with the First Folio's elaborate stage directions, read by Cornelius while the battle was performed in the remote distance upstage of him, to the disapproval of Robert Cushman: 'Here I quarrel with Mr Barton: the battle is a decisive factor in the action, and in the destinies of many of the characters, and . . . we need to get a good look at it' (*Observer*, 9 June 1974). Cushman is right. This sequence sags when either the battle or Posthumus's account of it is reduced or omitted, since it weakens the importance of Posthumus at the very moment that Shakespeare is building him up. And yet the traditional cuts do point to a peculiarity in construction here. It is odd that Shakespeare shows us a battle to whose elaboration the Folio directions bear witness, and then has Posthumus describe it in a detailed speech whose sustained vigour and energetic rhythms ensure that when it is included it makes a strong local effect. Only Robin Phillips's production at Stratford, Ontario in 1986 offered an explanation for this duplication. He presented the battle itself graphically, as the stage directions prescribe, and then suggested that Posthumus's account of it was there to make us reconsider it from the point of view of someone who had actually been through it. A natural psychological consequence of this traumatic experience was his dream, or in Phillips's interpretation nightmare, of Jupiter. This approach certainly made good sense of this tricky sequence from V.i to V.v.

The Jupiter scene itself raises a somewhat different problem. Whereas Shakespeare follows the virtuoso theatricality of the battle with language of equal impact, in Posthumus's description, Jupiter's descent is preceded by some very bizarre language spoken by the ghosts of Posthumus's family. Basically, they speak jog-trot 'fourteeners', a rhythm that was old-fashioned when Shakespeare wrote the play. Critics have often expressed incredulity that Shakespeare should have written so 'badly'; but this style may have had a specific dramatic function. Once again, Ovid casts light on the technique – not the original this time, but Arthur Golding's translation of 1567, which is written in just this metre. This, for instance, is how Golding renders the transformation of Philomel and her sister into birds:

So hovered they with wings indeed, of whom the one away
To woodward flies, the other still about the house doth stay.
(Book 6, 845-6)

Shakespeare had already affectionately parodied this metre in the play-within-the-play of *A Midsummer Night's Dream*; and he uses it again here to set Posthumus's vision off from the blank verse of the rest of the scene, so as to give the impression of a remote, perhaps quaint, antiquity – and also to emphasise that Posthumus is dreaming.

Perhaps, too, that element of wonder and astonishment that keeps recurring as the metamorphoses take place in Ovid and in Golding is relevant to the way an audience should respond to this scene. Sometimes modern audiences, unused to this particular kind of spectacle, giggle; but their usual response consists of gasps of amazement and even rounds of applause, which certainly happened in William Gaskill's production at Stratford-upon-Avon, and in both Jean Gascon's and Robin Phillips's at Stratford, Ontario, on a mock-Elizabethan stage whose upper level is well suited to such sudden, spectacular appearances. Amazement and applause are appropriate responses to the showmanship of the scene.

When Posthumus wakes and reads the obscure but encouraging prophecy that Jupiter has left with him, the language returns to 'normal' as Posthumus expresses himself in that terse, compressed, difficult style characteristic of much of Shakespeare's late verse:

'Tis still a dream, or else such stuff as madmen
Tongue, and brain not; either both, or nothing,
Or senseless speaking, or a speaking such
As sense cannot untie. (V.v.239-42)

But he adds that, obscure though it is, it seems oddly like the way his own life has turned out:

Be what it is,
The action of my life is like it. (V.v.242-3)

This speech makes explicit what was strongly implied by the earlier scenes; the theatrical virtuosity, and the strangeness it represents, emphasise 'the basic human situation'. Elijah Moshinsky took this speech as the key to his television interpretation: 'it's exactly how the play should be. . . . Shakespeare is saying the confusion of the play is like life: it's bizarre and emotionally

[20]

penetrating and psychologically intense. And very lifelike' (BBC edition, p. 26). It is because audiences sense this that the play works so well in performance.

One further aspect of these three scenes in modern interpretations should be mentioned. All three are linked by one central fact: the heroine or hero lies asleep during part or all of them. This has led several directors to interpret the bizarre situations as dreams, or nightmares, so that in the moments of extremest theatrical virtuosity, the action on stage can emerge as the externalisation of those dreams. In the modern production where their theatricality had the greatest impact, William Gaskill's in 1962, they certainly seemed to belong together. Each episode was prefaced by a prolonged pause, as Innogen fell asleep in her bedroom and Posthumus in his prison, or as Innogen awoke from her drugged sleep to a kind of half-sleeping, half-waking state beside Cloten's corpse. There was no doubt that the weird events were actually happening, but there was the implication that they were a kind of dream as well. What was simply a strong hint here became a central motif in Elijah Moshinsky's television version, and in Robin Phillips's Ontario one.

The case has been put most explicitly by Moshinsky in the BBC edition. He says that there are two levels of action in the play, an objective and a subjective level, 'and the subjective level is like a series of nightmares. One of the nightmares, for example, is Giacomo coming out of the trunk. I get the impression that Giacomo so disturbs Innogen . . . that she in a sense has a nightmare about the presence of Giacomo which we know, objectively, to be true.' He also argues that Innogen's scene by Cloten's corpse is another nightmare 'which is a kind of therapy for her. Then there is also Posthumus and his dream of Jupiter – I think the play centres round these therapeutic dreams which are internal to the character' (p. 17). This interpretation receives textual support, at least in the last two scenes, from the fact that the characters themselves see what is happening to them in these terms. As Innogen wakes beside Cloten's body, she assumes, in her semi-drugged state, that she must still be dreaming:

> I hope I dream,
> For so I thought I was a cavekeeper,
> And cook to honest creatures. But 'tis not so.
> 'Twas but a bolt of nothing, shot of nothing,
> Which the brain makes of fumes. (IV.ii.299-303)

And after reading the tablet left by Jupiter, Posthumus comments:

> 'Tis still a dream, or else such stuff as madmen
> Tongue, and brain not. (V.v.239-40)

Moshinsky's interpretation of the bedchamber scene has less secure textual support for the obvious reason that Innogen remains asleep during it; but there is certainly a strong hint that she may be dreaming about rape since she has been reading the tale of Tereus, reaching the point where 'Philomel gave up' just before falling asleep (II.ii.46).

As for the Jupiter scene, Brian Gibbons claims that 'nobody who has seen the episode performed could think Jupiter's presence other than supremely actual' (*Shakespeare Survey 39*, 1987, p. 218). This assumes that all performances of the scene are alike. Since in fact they vary so greatly, from the 'supremely actual' the merest hint, what people think in the theatre depends upon what they see performed. But in any case William Gaskill, whose Jupiter in 1962 was the most solid, 'supremely actual' of all, simultaneously suggested by imaginative staging and lighting that Posthumus was dreaming, and there is clear gain from an interpretation which links these three virtuoso scenes. It helps to bind the play together, and to give it a kind of unity in performance.

From the seventeenth to the twentieth century

Before describing some major modern productions in detail, it may be useful to place them in the context of the play's theatrical fortunes since the seventeenth century. Although the dramatisation of Cymbeline as a prince of peace may have been designed to appeal to James I, there is in fact no record that he ever saw the play. But his son Charles I certainly saw it in 1634 and we know what he thought of it: the Master of the Revels reports that it was 'well liked by the king'. When *Cymbeline* reappeared on the Restoration stage, it did so in the radically re-written shape of Thomas D'Urfey's *The Injured Princess or the Fatal Wager*. This version replaced the original from 1682 until 1738. In 1761, David Garrick staged what was basically Shakespeare's play at Drury Lane, and played Posthumus, which was one of his favourite parts; but, like many productions until recent times, he omitted the Jupiter scene and drastically curtailed the ending. From this point the play seems to have become very popular: it was given in London almost every year from 1761 until 1787, when the celebrated actress Sarah Siddons played Innogen.

In the nineteenth century, by contrast, there seems to have been more enthusiasm for the play in the study – notably from Tennyson, Hazlitt, and Swinburne – than on the stage, where it was given much less frequently than in the eighteenth century. And when it did appear, it was weighed down by elaborate archaeological realism. When, for example, Charles Kemble staged it at Covent Garden in 1827 (and, following Garrick's example, played Posthumus), he used detailed pictorial sets by the Grieves brothers. One of their designs is reproduced in *Shakespeare Survey 20*, 1967, Plate V.A. It shows a mini-Stonehenge in the centre of the stage: a cromlech surrounded by a circle of small stones. In the foreground is an iron-age hut, with shields and a harp. The relevance of all this to the theatrical requirements of Shakespeare's text is hard to demonstrate. But similar elaboration characterised the designs of Laurence Alma-Tadema for the most famous production of the nineteenth century, Henry Irving's at the Lyceum Theatre, London, in 1896 with Irving himself as Giacomo and Ellen Terry as Innogen.

Ellen Terry exchanged letters with Bernard Shaw during the rehearsal period. Shaw affected to despise *Cymbeline* and even wrote a jokey new version of the final scene, which was actually performed in London in 1937. And yet in his letter to Ellen Terry of 6 September 1896, he showed remarkable insight into what he called the 'dramatic cunning' of Innogen's scene by Cloten's corpse which reveals such a grasp of how the speech works in theatrical terms that it is worth quoting at length:

> you wake up, you sit up, half awake, and think you are asking the way to Milford Haven . . . You lie down to sleep again, and in doing so touch the body of Cloten, whose head (or no head) is presumably muffled in a cloak. In your dim, half asleep funny state of consciousness, you still have the idea that you mustn't go to bed with anybody else but Posthumus, and you say 'But soft, no bedfellow.' Then in rousing yourself sufficiently to get away from this vaguely apprehended person, you awaken a little more at this very odd, dreamlike thing, that the bedfellow is covered with flowers. You take up a flower, still puzzly-dreamy, and look curiously at it. It is *bloody*, and then in an instant you are broad awake – 'Oh gods and

goddesses!' etc. But it is quite clear that you must not know that this 'bloody man' is headless, as that would utterly spoil the point later on. He looks simply as if he had swathed his head in his cloak to sleep in. . . . When you utter the prayer 'If there be / Yet left in heaven as small a drop of pity / As a wren's eye, feared gods, a part of it', I suppose you kneel and cover your eyes with your hands in the hope that when you remove them your prayer will be answered and the nightmare gone. You take down your hands and dare to look again. 'The dream's here still. Even when I wake it is / Without me as within me; not imagined – felt.'

This detailed account of the moment-to-moment development of the speech anticipates the ways in which modern actresses have handled it, especially Innogen's half-sleeping, half-waking state, and the fact that she only gradually discovers that the corpse is headless. But Shaw also had a problem with the speech. After his fine analysis up to 'not imagined – felt', he adds:

Now in the text, what follows is 'A headless man!' This is what I cannot understand. . . . For see how it plays if you omit it. Your attention is caught by the garment of Posthumus; you go on with the recognition step by step . . . ; at last you lift the cloak to see the face, and then – 'Murder in Heaven!' you go tearing, screaming, raging mad, and rave your way to the swoon as best you can . . . But if you leave in the words 'A headless man' the sequel is spoiled, and you are . . . surprised at finding no face on a man who, as you have already observed, has lost his whole head. (Christopher St John, ed., *Ellen Terry and Bernard Shaw: a Correspondence*, 1931, pp. 45-6)

Shaw has certainly identified a problem here. As a practical man of the theatre, he realises the need to grade the speech emotionally, and not to let rip too soon, a point made several times by directors and actresses in the following chapters; but the recognition 'A headless man' does seem to necessitate the release of a headlong flood of passion, and that is how it has frequently been played. Yet there are other ways of handling 'A headless man' and the identification of the garments which meet Shaw's objection, as will emerge in considering Vanessa Redgrave's and Geraldine James's performances later. Ellen Terry seems to have benefited from Shaw's tuition; hers was the most famous Innogen before Peggy Ashcroft's, whose performance at the Old Vic, London, in 1932 was a first sketch for the outstanding performance she gave a quarter of a century later at Stratford-upon-Avon, described in detail in the next chapter.

Meanwhile *Cymbeline* became part of the vogue for presenting

Shakespeare in modern dress when Barry Jackson invited M. K. Ayliff to stage it at the Birmingham Repertory Theatre in 1923. In this production, Giacomo proposed the wager at a dinner party in evening dress: here Jackson and Ayliff anticipated Robin Phillips's staging at Stratford, Ontario by over sixty years, and whereas Phillips's updating represented a nostalgia for the 1930s and 1940s, theirs was in genuinely *modern* dress: this enabled them to dress Arviragus and Guiderius simply, in flannel shirts and socks, rather than taking refuge in the weird surrealistic image of the noble savage adopted by Phillips. Most productions this century, however, have been at Stratford-upon-Avon, six revivals before Peter Hall's of 1957. None of them seems to have been particularly notable either in staging or in individual performances, except for Paul Scofield's Cloten in 1946, which anticipated several more recent interpreters in suggesting that the character cannot be simply dismissed as a 'clotpoll'. Ben Iden Payne's 1937 version was the first to show the influence of the Jacobean court and the masque: behind a formal archway in the style of Inigo Jones were set decorative versions of Innogen's bedchamber, Belarius's cave, and so on.

Michael Benthall directed the play at Stratford in 1949 and at the Old Vic in 1956, and his two productions represented the extremes of elaboration and simplicity in staging *Cymbeline*. Like Payne in 1937, Benthall in 1949 gave the play a basic architectural frame, but in a very different style from Payne's: between two massive Norman arches, a series of painted cloths suggested the different scenes: Cymbeline's palace was evoked by perspectives of colonnades and vast flights of steps stretching far away into the distance, Jupiter by a circular formation of clouds and the eagle's wings and head, in the centre of which the actor appeared to deliver, not Jupiter's own speech, but the prophecy that in the text he leaves with Posthumus. This vast, gloomy staging harked back to the nineteenth century; most critics felt that it made 'heavy weather' of the play, and longed for a 'lighter' treatment.

Benthall seems to have agreed with them, for in 1956, according to Mary Clarke in her book about the Old Vic season,

> there was no setting at all, not even a stark and permanent one. The figures emerged from darkness and into darkness disappeared. The shifting pageant gained miraculously in simplicity; changes in the texture and colour of the lighting suggested quite clearly the changes from sunny Italy to misty Britain, from sea-air at dawn near Milford Haven to the midnight quietness of Innogen's bedroom. This method

> succeeded most of all in making the audience listen to the verse,
> listen as closely as any Jacobean audience, and somehow the dark-
> ness around the characters helped this concentration of attention.
> (*Shakespeare at the Old Vic*, 1957, n.p.)

Mary Clarke gives several examples of this concentration upon what characters are thinking and feeling: in the confrontation between Giacomo and Innogen, 'the reaction of each character to the other's every word was almost spotlit for the audience'; in the bedroom scene, only the bed and the trunk were lit, thus focusing upon Innogen and upon Giacomo's response to her; in the burial scene, the speaking of the dirge 'had a quality of wonderful stillness and sadness'. And Muriel St Clare Byrne in *Shakespeare Quar terly* provided another example: 'when Arviragus returned with the sup-posedly dead Fidele in his arms the lighting, the darkness and the close grouping all combined to give one perfect, golden, silent moment' (*Shakespeare Quarterly*, VIII, 1957, p. 463).

This suggests that the production's simplicity and concentration had the advantage of drawing attention to a major aspect of Shakespeare's technique in this play by isolating and spotlighting individual moments of powerful emotion. In the process, Benth-all's version provided further evidence of specific theatrical qual-ities that have also emerged in other productions: the poignancy of Arviragus's 'The bird is dead' as he appears carrying Innogen in his arms; the effectiveness of the Welsh scenes and the impact of the strong performances of Belarius and the princes, in defiance of academic disapproval; and what Mary Clarke called Barbara Jefford's sense of 'exquisite happiness . . . in the discovery of her brothers' at the end. Clarke also praised Barbara Jefford for playing Innogen with 'just the right lightness of touch', something that was clearly absent from Benthall's previous version and, so far as one can judge, from the heavy-handedness of the elaborate stagings prior to that. Lightness of touch is an apt quality in performing *Cymbeline*, since it helps to emphasise the theatrical virtuosity of the play. It has been sought after by several directors, especially by William Gaskill in 1962, and by Peter Hall who, during rehear-sals of his second production of the play at the National Theatre in 1988, constantly asked his actors for fleetness and lightness. He first directed the play thirty years earlier, and his 1957 production is the subject of the next chapter.

CHAPTER II

'First and foremost a romance': Peter Hall's production, Stratford-upon-Avon, 1957

In a lecture given at Stratford-upon-Avon at the time of his production of *Cymbeline* there, Peter Hall claimed that the play was 'first and foremost a romance' (quoted in *The Times*, 26 August 1957). A difficulty about this term, as Stanley Wells points out in his article on 'Shakespeare and Romance', is that 'it means so much that often it means nothing at all' (in J. R. Brown and Bernard Harris, eds., *Later Shakespeare*, 1966, p. 49). Wells explains that romance as a genre cannot be described by 'formal characteristics' but rather by 'a recognizable attitude towards the subject-matter. Romancers delight in the marvellous; quite often this involves the supernatural; generally the characters are larger than life size.' In romance, as in folklore, we should no more ask rational questions about character 'than we should question the motives of Cinderella or examine the psychology of the three bears' (p. 53). That Peter Hall was taking 'romance' in this sense is confirmed by his further remark that the staging was to be as 'archetypal and fairy storyish as possible'.

Seizing upon the fact that *Cymbeline* combines ancient Britain, classical Rome, medieval Italy, and seventeenth-century England, Hall presented a visual mixture which alluded to all of those periods, so that costumes from one era deliberately clashed with those from another. The designer was Lila de Nobili, an Italian painter whose sensuously elaborate, richly pictorial style might be regarded as a modern equivalent of the extravagant designs of the seventeenth-century masque. Her set was as allusive as her costumes, fusing the play's various locations into one huge permanent structure that simultaneously showed a Renaissance interior, church towers, a central stone archway that could also do duty as a cave, winding paths, and dark overhanging woods. Much of it was practicable, with its tall stained-glass windows behind which light glinted mysteriously, its staircases, and its close forgotten ways: when Innogen arrived at Belarius's cave and said 'Here is a path to' t' (III.vi.18), she had one that she could use. This dark, shadowy world was framed by a proscenium consisting of two giant, solid oaks, apparently cast from local trees for maximum realism; like much of the architecture of the set, they were covered with ivy. But if this set alluded to most of the varied elements of the play, its sheer size and complexity ran the risk of overwhelming the actors; and if its inspiration was the seventeenth-century masque, its execution was closer to nineteenth-century romanticism.

In this review of the production, Kenneth Tynan offered a useful visual point of reference when he said that it resembled 'a Grimm fable transmuted by the Cocteau of "La Belle et La Bête"' (*Observer*, 7 July 1957). Cocteau's classic film version (1946) of the legend of Beauty and the Beast makes a particularly apt comparison. Like this *Cymbeline*, it is memorable for lavish pictorial effects. The castle is shrouded by dark woods; inside the castle hall, the candelabra take the form of live arms emerging from the wall, and the eyes of the statues suddenly open and follow the characters around. These eerie touches are characteristic of the film's grotesque fairytale world. In its visual elaboration, it seems like a twentieth-century version of nineteenth-century stage design, and that was very much the impression of this *Cymbeline* also.

Tynan's review provided details of how this design worked in practical terms. It took us, he said,

> straight into the world of momentous fantasy where the play can flourish. Posthumus . . . is a perfect white-clad knight, the Queen . . . an Arthurian enchantress. Helmets gleam and threaten from high hillsides, and all the costumes are silvery, bulrushy, or glaucous green. All but [those] for the Romans, who wear crimson and gold: the massed advance of those embossed and glittering shields makes a stunning visual impact.

At the start of the play, there was a gauze curtain between the two oaks, decorated with a baroque image of winged youths, smiling in welcome and about to part the curtains. When the curtains actually did part, they revealed, as Roy Walker reported, not only the two gentlemen but 'a score of fantastic fairy-tale figures' *Shakespeare Survey* 11, 1958, p. 134). In this context, the principals were presented as archetypes, especially the Queen, instantly recognisable as a wicked stepmother in her black robes with their overlay of black lace and net. With her 'dead white face and splayed white fingers', Walker said, she looked 'like some arcane transformation of Titania into Lady Macbeth', a phrase that not only described this Queen vividly but also caught the play's own range of reference. Cymbeline, the archetypal monarch, wore white and gold robes trimmed with ermine. Their robes and their spiky primitive crowns established these two characters as a mythical king and queen from the remote past. Giacomo appeared to be an Italianate villain in black, Posthumus and Innogen an archetypal hero and heroine in white, silver, and blue.

This treatment divided press reaction right down the middle, as two representative reviews make clear. T. C. Worsley in the *New Statesman* of 20 July 1957 and the anonymous critic ('N.T.') for the *Leamington Spa Courier* of 5 July 1957 provided equally accurate and informative accounts of what happened on stage, but they held diametrically-opposed views about the value of what they described. Worsley thought the production 'admirable', N.T. 'a comprehensive failure'. Worsley felt that 'Lila de Nobili's delightful sets conjure up enchantment', N.T. that the designer was given 'so free a hand to proliferate romance that, under the weight of all her fabrications, the life of the play . . . is altogether quenched'. And this reviewer went on to raise an important issue about the play itself. To interpret it as a romance, he argued, 'leaves out nearly everything of value in the play'. He is drawing attention here to the way in which Shakespeare's treatment of the story, and especially the language, complicates the initial impression of simple stereotypes. The production's approach enabled Cymbeline himself to be played neutrally, a remote legendary figure, as the reviewer grudgingly admitted: 'Robert Harris played the King with a stiff dignity that was neither helpful nor otherwise to a production in need of a strong hand.' But although the Queen could have been given a similar remoteness, this reviewer agreed with most others that Joan Miller brought great variety to it: she 'found exactly the tone for the savage–farcical part of the Queen – her modulation in a breath from her murderous hate of

Pisanio to the innocent charm of her supervision of the posy-gatherers drew laughter of the right sort – and she was splendid in her mockery of the Romans'. This performance both fitted the romance convention of the production and demonstrated that that convention, in her case, did not necessarily prevent the range of the part from being expressed.

Nor in the case of Cloten: the romance approach might have limited him to what Guiderius calls him, 'an arrogant piece of flesh' (IV.ii.128), a simpleton with too much money and power. His satin court costume initially gave this impression, but Clive Revill went well beyond that in a skilful performance that was widely admired. Robert Speaight's inspired description of him as 'a cretinous Infante out of Velasquez' (*Shakespeare on the Stage*, 1973, p. 252) exactly caught this Cloten's combination of drooping lip and courtly splendour. But such men were also dangerous, and Revill expressed the character's violence by means of a verbal mannerism suggested by Belarius's reference to 'the snatches in his voice/ And burst of speaking' (IV.ii.106-7), so that a phrase like 'She hath despised me rejoicingly, and I'll be merry in my revenge' (III.v.144-5) became a furious outburst. But it was not *just* an outburst: Revill brought out something else suggested in that line. The link between Innogen's 'rejoicing' as she despised him and his correspondingly 'merry' revenge implies a man not wholly cretinous, not entirely unable to make mental connections. But Revill brilliantly implied that this mental capacity came and went; when, for instance, he was told that 'it is not fit your lordship should undertake every companion that you give offence to', Revill replied doubtfully 'N-no, I know *that*', sensing criticism but unsure exactly what that criticism might be (II.i.26-8). His delivery ranged from those 'bursts of speaking' to a slow, steady attempt to work out what he was saying in the process of saying it, and this fully revealed the tortuous thought-process in 'if thou wouldst not be a villain but do me true service . . . that is, what villainy soe'er I bid thee do, to perform it directly and truly – I would think thee an honest man' (III.v.108-13). The contradictions here were made to seem utterly logical to Cloten himself.

By the use of this logic, Revill demonstrated how the man who is a cretin in some ways can also rise to flights of imaginative sadistic fancy. The full range of part and performance emerged in his soliloquy when he arrived in Wales dressed in Posthumus's clothes (IV.i.). It began with confident vanity – 'How fit his garments serve me!' – but the mental uncertainty, and the need to work things out, returned with the wordplay on 'fit' and 'fits': 'Why should his mistress, who was made by him that made the tailor, not be fit too? – the rather – saving reverence of the word – for 'tis said a woman's fitness comes by fits.' Working out this wordplay cost him a great effort, and he seemed exhausted and uncertain again as he spoke the last word. But he rallied at the realisation that 'the lines of my body are as well drawn' as Post-humus's. Then a new reflection struck him – 'What mortality is!' – and this led into his most imaginative flight:

> Posthumus, thy head which now is growing upon thy shoulders shall within this hour be off, thy mistress enforced, thy garments cut to pieces before thy face; and all this done, spurn her home to her father –

but as he reached the climax of this plan, he suddenly checked himself, as it dawned on him that this scheme might have its problems –

> who may haply be a *little* angry for my so rough usage –

but that could of course be overcome by the intervention of the Queen. And the soliloquy ended in arrogance as it began: 'the fellow *dares* not deceive *me*'. The variety of Revill's performance in this speech indicated the range and interest of the role, a character who is very much more than a 'clotpoll'. And like all good Clotens, he was amazed, in the exchange with Guiderius, to meet someone who was entirely unimpressed at being told he was the Queen's son, Cloten: 'Art not *afeared?*' (IV. ii. 96). Throughout the perfor-mance, this Cloten expressed a recurrent frustration that somehow all his rank, power, and ambitious schemes were not always achieving what they should for him. After Innogen's vigorous rejec-tion of him, for example, his last line moved from indignation – 'His meanest garment?' – to a puzzled, frustrated 'Well': he couldn't quite see either why he had to suffer such setbacks or what was to be done about them.

This frustration is, in the text, matched by Posthumus in a simil-arly angry response to Innogen: 'I'll do *something*' (II.iv.149). The connection between Posthumus's and Cloten's frustration and vio-lent threats to Innogen could not emerge in this produciton, how-ever, for despite such a complex Cloten, Posthumus was presented merely as a romantic hero. Richard Johnson tried to establish this image by a breathy delivery, sighing out 'My queen, my mistress!'

at the start. But such an approach did not allow the part to develop, and provided no resource for dealing with either the wager scene or, crucially, Posthumus's soliloquy in II.v. when he thinks Innogen has betrayed him. Johnson delivered it in glossy tones with a kind of built-in reverberation that brought 'O vengeance, vengeance!' perilously close to rant. This generalised, all-purpose technique dissuaded inquiry into the possible implications of his reference to Innogen's rosy pudency that 'might well have warmed old Saturn', and ignored the modulations of tone. He completely missed the grossness of imagining Giacomo 'like a full-acorned boar' crying 'O!' and mounting Innogen; he spluttered through the cynicism about women with its obsessive repetitions –

> flattering, hers; deceiving, hers;
> Lust and rank thoughts, hers, hers; revenges, hers –

and he concluded the soliloquy by delivering the final line 'The very devils cannot plague them better' with a slow, hammered emphasis, as if it were the climax of the speech rather than a deliberate anti-climax, a single line thrown in after the apparently concluding couplet.

This seemed almost an object-lesson in how *not* to bring off this speech; yet the performance was much admired by reviewers. The explanation, I think, is that such glossy tones were much used in the 1950s to present romantic and tragic characters; it was almost expected that actors should assume a kind of poetry voice which prevented too close an investigation into the rhythms, the language, and hence the meaning and motivation of their roles. It was in fact against this kind of verbal varnish that Peter Hall himself reacted when he became director of the Stratford theatre in 1960, and encouraged his new permanent company to probe more deeply into the meaning of what they were saying than was possible in the *ad hoc* conditions prevailing in 1957. He succeeded so well, and so quickly, that by 1962, when the next production of *Cymbeline* was given, Patrick Allen and his director William Gaskill were able to achieve a much more inquiring and coherent account of this soliloquy and of Posthumus's part as a whole.

A Posthumus who is a wronged hero needs a Giacomo who is a diabolic villain – and this Geoffrey Keen in 1957 did not provide. Robert Speaight, remarking that in this play 'we are never really within hailing distance of tragedy' said of this Giacomo that 'it was clever not to have reminded us of Iago' (*The Tablet*, 16 September 1957). Keen managed this to some extent by resorting frequently to mocking laughter, especially when tauntingly asking Posthumus to check whether Innogen mentions in her letter that she has sent him the bracelet: 'She writes so to you, doth she?' (II.iv.105). The bedroom scene defined the limitations of the interpretation. This was one scene where the set brought positive advantages: its shady chiaroscuro, and its simultaneous suggestion of a Renaissance interior and of woodland, helped to focus the language of the scene. In such a world it seemed quite natural for Giacomo to evoke Tarquin, Philomel, and the crimson drops in the bottom of a cowslip all within the space of a few lines. Even so, Keen missed some of the implications. There was no menace in his reference to Tarquin, and even the comparison of Innogen to Venus in the exclamation 'Cytherea!' was boomed out, syllable by syllable. The manner hinted at irony, but not very clearly. Again, there was a suggestion of the comic in that the bracelet stubbornly refused to be moved – 'Come off, (*slight pause; more emphatic:*) come off!' – but these undertones did not fully surface until this Giacomo chuckled after 'the leaf's turned down / Where Philomel gave up'. But what did the chuckle express? Was it irony, in that Innogen was being betrayed like Philomel, despite not being raped like her? Or that Giacomo saw the whole wager simply as a game that he had won by sleight of hand? The performance did not seem to have made up its mind where it was going. It was certainly not tragic, but nor was it sufficiently lightweight and humorous to bring out the sophisticated irony so expertly presented by Eric Porter in the following Stratford production.

This unfocused Giacomo and Posthumus deprived the wager scene of natural flow and inevitable development, as Peter Hall seemed to acknowledge by uncharacteristically injecting melodramatic incident into the scene. As Posthumus noisily threatened Giacomo with 'a repulse', Giacomo half-drew his sword, so that Philario had hastily to intervene: 'Gentlemen, enough of this' (I.iv.116-18). The tension thus artificially whipped up was then relaxed into forced laughter only to be whipped up again as Giacomo returned to his theme. This abrupt stopping and starting, together with Posthumus's ranting and Giacomo's hollow booming, gave no sense of what these two characters were like or what the wager was really about.

The uncertain handling recurred in Posthumus's later scenes, beginning with his repentance and culminating in his vision of

Jupiter. The sequence was drastically curtailed – perhaps, again, in acknowledgement of the limitations of this Posthumus. His repentant soliloquy was shorn of its first sixteen lines, beginning at 'I am brought hither / Among th' Italian gentry' (V.i.17-18), so that the crucial point that Posthumus has forgiven Innogen while still believing her guilty was obscured. After it, the Roman army formed a glittering shield-wall and drove the Britons downstage, where they all fell down in unison and in slow motion. T. C. Worsley thought that this 'piece of pure convention' was 'somewhat absurd but charmingly absurd and within the style of the whole'. Perhaps; but what it missed was the element of elaborate spectacle implied by the Folio's detailed stage direction, and also the reason for such elaboration – the need to re-establish Posthumus as a heroic or quasi-heroic character. The problem was compounded by the omission of his entire battle narration, and the extensive abbreviation of his other speeches.

For his vision, he lay manacled on the floor in the centre of the stage, surrounded by other Roman prisoners at the edges. In this way, the multiple set took on the further dimension of a prison, with the lighting focused on Posthumus. In keeping with the pictorial, decorative bias of the production, the appearance of Jupiter was not a physical descent but an image painted on to a gauze. As the general lighting dimmed, this gauze was flown in behind the sleeping Posthumus, and his ghostly family was, initially, silhouetted against it as they surrounded him. When the moment for Jupiter's descent arrived, the gauze was fully lit, revealing a formal golden image of Jupiter on his eagle in the clouds throwing a thunderbolt. The original intention may not, however, have been purely decorative. It was rumoured that Hall had wanted to fly Jupiter down, but that the eagle, once made, was too heavy to fly and so the gauze was substituted. However that may be, it was left to the next production in 1962 to bring off this effect properly. Even so, Hall's treatment made points about the scene. The ghosts used a weird, bleating chant which set them off from the mortals and went some way towards suggesting Shakespeare's purpose in using those jog-trot 'fourteeners': they evoked quaintness, remoteness, antiquity. This made a proper contrast with Jupiter's speech, delivered sonorously by Mark Dignam over loudspeakers: this was a vigorous, testy god who was not prepared to put up with any nonsense from 'mortal flies'. But then Posthumus's waking speech was reduced from twenty-eight lines to six, and the scene sagged again.

Although the sequence was so drastically shortened, this production obviously included more of it than was usual at the time, since several critics commented in surprise at 'a rather greater allowance than usual of the supernatural' (*Leamington Spa Courier*, 5 July 1957). But it was not enough. The flimsy gauze, like the stylised battle, did not supply the elaborate physical manoeuvres required at this point, so that the Jupiter episode did not emerge as the climax and turning-point of Posthumus's fortunes.

Mark Dignam doubled Jupiter with Pisanio, to whom he brought a characteristic vein of irony that intensified rather than questioned the character's integrity. When handling the Queen or Cloten or even Innogen, this Pisanio combined an impression of much put-upon hard work with a goodness that, as even the Queen recognised, was 'not to be shaked' (I.v.76). Like other reviewers, T. C. Worsley acclaimed 'perfection so easy and yet commanding, an absolute rightness in every inflection, every sly characterful glance, however slight'. These sly glances were sometimes exchanged conspiratorially with Innogen, sometimes with an ironic eye on the audience, notably as he clinched the couplet to the departing Queen,

> But when to my good lord I prove untrue,
> I'll choke myself – there's all I'll do for you (I.v.86-7)

as he clapped a battered trilby on to his head and stomped off stage. The image of a trusty old retainer presented here has been the one adopted by most performers of this part. The character does not invite great variety of interpretation – or so it seemed until an inquiring production at The Other Place in Stratford broke the mould thirty years later.

However much they disagreed about the production as a whole, the two representative reviews I quoted earlier concurred about the success of the pastoral scenes. T. C. Worsley related this success to what he saw as Hall's general achievement in staging and design: 'he seems to have looked with all the imagination of which he was capable at the play itself to find the principle which will give it unity' and found it in 'the point of balance where the pastoral simplicity and courtly intrigue are parts of a logical whole'. In the pastoral scenes the set made its greatest contribution, since much of it – the oaks that framed the proscenium, the winding paths and overhanging woods, and the predominating colour scheme of grey, green and brown – harmonised beautifully with language which draws so much on the natural world. This raises the important question of how far a production should physically reflect the details of the writing. This is not a question of a literal-minded scene-painting of actual locations in the nineteenth-century manner so much as embodying the atmosphere and implications of the language. Nor is it a matter of simple right and wrong; the productions described in detail here took very different attitudes to this question. But one advantage of Hall's method was that there was a clear connection between what the characters were saying and the surroundings in which they appeared.

In such a context, lines like Arviragus's

> What should we speak of
> When we are old as you? When we shall hear
> The rain and wind beat dark December, how,
> In this our pinching cave, shall we discourse
> The freezing hours away? (III.iii.35-9)

seemed to rise naturally from the world created by the production, and to gain additional impact from that setting; so, still more, did Arviragus's 'With fairest flowers' speech of consolation to Innogen, especially the detail about the 'furred moss' which will protect her corpse from the winter. Even the editor of the new Arden edition, who had begun by thinking the princes embarrassing and unconvincing parts, modified his opinion after seeing this staging: 'the very considerable difficulties of the Cave scenes were overcome by emphasising the comedy and, at times, the poignancy' (1960 and subsequent editions, p. 219). The comedy to which he refers occurred, for example, when the princes ribbed Belarius affectionately about his 'stiff age' (III.iii.32), and the poignancy obviously in the burial scene.

The *Leamington Courier* reviewer who so disliked the production as a whole agreed with Worsley and other reviewers about these scenes: 'Even in the smother of this production, single scenes survived: not much was lost, for instance, of the poignant simplicity of Arviragus's 'The bird is dead / That we have made so much on', standing at the mouth of the cave with Innogen in his arms.' 'Smother' is one way of describing the effect of this production; another is to notice that it brought out an essential aspect of the technique of the play, the way in which it emphasises isolated moments by making them stand out from contexts that are often complicated in terms of plot and narrative. This reviewer added that 'much of the success of these pastoral scenes was due to Cyril Luckham's sensible Belarius' – further testimony to the effectiveness of this role in performance.

The real distinction of this production, however, was Peggy Ashcroft's Innogen. She, above all, demonstrated the complexity of what starts off as a fairy-tale role, as she released the full emotional range of the part. She achieved this largely by vocal means. It has often been remarked that an actress whose voice is clear rather than especially beautiful in itself nevertheless always achieves results of outstanding musical beauty. Thirty years after he had worked with her in *Cymbeline*, Peter Hall defined this 'musicality':

> She has a magnificent voice, trained and developed over many years, and she has . . . a particular idiosyncratic way of making Shakespeare beat rhythmically, keeping the line. At the end of a line when Peggy is speaking Shakespeare she slightly stresses the last couple of words or last word of the line. This defines the end of the line, gives the linear structure and makes it move on with great energy.
> (Quoted in Robert Tanitch, *Ashcroft*, 1987)

There were two particularly good examples of this technique in her Innogen. The first was the way in which she emphasised the last word of a line in order to convey her indignation at Giacomo's attempted seduction:

> The King my father shall be made acquainted
> Of thy assault. If he shall think it fit (*slight pause*)
> A saucy stranger in his court to *mart* (*very emphatic*)
> As in a Romish stew, and to expound (*slight pause, to prepare for:*)
> His *beastly mind* to us, he hath a court
> He little cares for, and a daughter who
> He not respects at all. (I.vi.150-6)

The line endings were marked by emphatic pauses or by slight hesitations, directing the audience's attention to the point of the next line; and yet there was no sense of a verse-speaking exercise. As she always does, Peggy Ashcroft used the verse structure to communicate the meaning: here, Innogen's aristocratic sense of outrage. Her exact achievement may be made clearer by comparison with what happens when an actress fails to make use of the technical means Shakespeare has provided to help her. At this point in the BBC television version, Helen Mirren breathlessly gabbles the lines, conveying no sense of how Shakespeare has structured them. The impression is of petulant annoyance, rather than of a princess rebuking an unworthy suitor, simply because the implications of the verse structure are disregarded. Peggy Ashcroft observed them to great effect again in the famous lines about Britain:

> I' th' world's volume
> Our Britain seems as of it but not in't,
> In a great pool a swan's nest. Prithee, think
> There's livers out of Britain. (III.iv.138-41)

Her measured delivery here gave full value to the idea of the island of Britain floating in isolation like a swan's nest. Then, by lingering over the two words 'Prithee, think', she at once stressed the line-ending and invested it with a haunting nostalgia, partly for the kingdom she must leave, partly for the husband who seems to have betrayed her, one of those 'livers out of Britain'. Because she responds so directly to Shakespeare's lines, and builds her performances firmly upon them, Peggy Ashcroft's style has never dated during her long career. She achieves exquisite modulations from one mood to another with no apparent difficulty, and this was ideal for Innogen.

In her parting with Posthumus, for instance, she immediately caught the tenderness of Innogen's claim that she is

> not comforted to live
> But that there is this jewel in the world
> That I may see again. (I.i.91-3)

The simplicity of her style here was the more noticeable because of the contrast with Richard Johnson's breathy, sentimental attempt to play the romantic hero. There was the same simple directness, but in a sharper vein, when she confronted Giacomo:

> I pray you, sir,
> Deliver with *more openness* your answers
> To my demands. *Why* do you pity me? (I.vi.88-90)

Innogen has sometimes been thought gullible for being deceived by Giacomo; but Peggy Ashcroft made the excellent point that Innogen's only failing is to attribute to other people her own straightforwardness and integrity. Her openness of manner was at the furthest remove from the weird interpretation of this episode on BBC television by Helen Mirren, where the character is almost seduced by Giacomo. There was heartache in Peggy Ashcroft's 'My lord, I fear, / Has forgot Britain'; but however badly she thought Giacomo had behaved, she still retained the courtesy of the great lady in her graceful reply 'O, no, no!' (I.vi.200) when Giacomo said he had to leave the next day. This made another interesting contrast, this time with Judi Dench's performance at Stratford-upon-Avon in 1979, whose icy civility to Giacomo at this moment did not conceal intense dislike.

Not that Peggy Ashcroft's Innogen lacked a sharp tongue, for example in her response to Cloten when provoked beyond endurance, delivered very rapidly, dismissively:

> If you'll be patient, I'll no more be mad;
> That cures us both. (II.iii.100-1)

But in the next phrase, her natural courtesy returned:

> I am much sorry, sir,
> You put me to forget a lady's manners
> By being so verbal. (II.iii.101-3)

Her restraint here again contrasted with Helen Mirren's television performance, which responds to Cloten's taunts by making 'His meanest garment' suggestively taunting in reply; nor did Peggy Ashcroft snap at Pisanio with her 'Go and search' (II.iii. 146), as Helen Mirren does, but was characteristically considerate. Elsewhere, she ranged from ecstasy – 'O for a horse with *wings!*' (III.ii.48) – to a desolation of spirit the more moving because understated: 'Or in my life what comfort when I am / Dead to my husband' (III.iv.130-1). The *Times* reviewer caught some of this variety when he said that 'Peggy Ashcroft has the light movement and the youthfully ardent voice suited to the most richly dowered of all Shakespeare's heroines. Nor does she endanger the lady's graces by withholding from them the grace of humour' (3 July 1957). As so often in Shakespeare, humour is a means of intensifying gracefulness rather than endangering it; like most Innogens, Peggy Ashcroft made the most of the humorous potential of her first line in male disguise: 'I see a man's life is a tedious one' (III.vi.1).

Her handling of the scene by Cloten's corpse illuminates details of the text and suggests how carefully Shakespeare has used broken phrases to express Innogen's half-waking state, and her growing realisation of the realities of her situation. There was a long pause, as there usually is, before Innogen stirred; at 'I have gone all night' she sat up, but her next phrase, 'Faith, I'll lie down and sleep', was an attempt to exorcise the waking nightmare of sensing that there was a body beside her: 'But soft, no bedfellow!' Rather than looking straight at it, she picked up some of the flowers that had been strewn over the two of them; but as she said 'These flowers are like the pleasures of the world', she noticed that there was blood on her hand, from the flowers. This led naturally into the next line, 'This bloody man the care on't', as she nerved herself to look directly at the body and so registered the grim truth; she dropped the flowers and turned away, covering her eyes, at 'I hope I dream.' Certain now that she was not in fact dreaming, she caught the sharpness of pain expressed in the tiny image of 'as small a drop of pity / As a wren's eye', and the sense of living out a nightmare in 'Even when I wake it is / Without me as within me: not imagined, *felt*.' On 'felt', she lifted the cloak from the bloody neck and hastily covered it again. As she did so, she recognised the clothes: 'The garments of Posthumus?' From this point on, she played the speech in an increasing torrent of passion. At the climax, she put her hands to her face, and the blood on them from the flowers streaked her face, a convincing interpretation of 'Give colour to my pale cheek with thy blood'; she finally broke down in tears as she fell upon the body. This performance made the point that, however carefully an actress begins the speech, avoiding becoming too intense too soon, however skilfully she differentiates between half-sleep and waking, there comes a point in this speech when there is nothing for it but to pull all the stops out. A long silence followed the speech as it had begun it, before the bustling world broke in upon her private grief in the form of the Roman army. There was then another great contrast with the simplicity and pathos of Innogen's attempt to express her existence without her husband: 'I am nothing; or if not, / Nothing to be were better' (IV.ii.369-70).

Because this Innogen had expressed her pain and grief so convincingly, her happiness at the end seemed all the greater. Partly this was done with words – 'Why did you throw your wedded lady from you?' (V.vi.262), very tender – but partly by other means. T. C. Worsley described the moment: 'Dame Peggy can do some things better than any actress living, some of them, too, quite simple things (or so they might seem), like the little run forward to reveal herself to her husband in the final recognition scene.' This makes the point that an Innogen has to express what must be an overwhelming reaction on discovering that Posthumus is in fact alive; she must inevitably respond with an ecstasy and amazement to counterbalance the agony that she experienced on thinking him dead. Shakespeare has given her no line with which to express this; the actress has to do it for herself. But then Posthumus strikes her down. When she recovers, she rebukes Pisanio: 'Dangerous fellow, hence. / Breathe not where princes are' (V.vi.239-40). There is obviously an aristocratic grandeur about this phrase, since Cymbeline immediately recognises 'the tune of Innogen' as he had not done earlier when he heard her speak as 'Fidele'. Peggy Ashcroft conveyed that, too. I have seen several fine Innogens – as Robert Cushman puts it, 'the role seems to make a princess out of anyone who plays it' (*Observer*, 22 December 1974) – but none of them has equalled her exceptional achievement in demonstrating the full potential of the role. T. C. Worsley concluded that her art carries the audience 'into the very nerve centres whence the tears (whether of sorrow or relief) spring' – and in the process she drew attention to something essential about the play itself: the capacity of the language to touch the audience's 'nerve centres', chiefly in Innogen's lines, but also in other people's response to her, in Arviragus's flower speech, the princes' dirge, and Giacomo's tribute in the bedroom.

If critical response to this production was divided, audience response was in general enthusiastic, as it usually is to this play in performance. The *Times* reviewer remarked that 'the Stratford audience tonight appeared greatly to enjoy this treatment' (3 July 1957), and T. C. Worsley in a second article pointed out that 'at Stratford . . . on the hottest of summer afternoons . . . hundreds of school children were discovering how the texts they might find dull and dusty in the classroom glow with a magic life on the stage' (*New Statesman*, 13 July 1957).

CHAPTER III

'Theatrical largesse':
William Gaskill's production,
Stratford-upon-Avon, 1962

It would be hard to imagine a greater visual contrast than that between the scenic elaboration of Peter Hall's *Cymbeline* and the next production at Stratford-upon-Avon five years later, when William Gaskill devised a staging of the utmost visual simplicity which threw a brilliant spotlight upon the text. This contrast reflected a significant development in production style at Stratford. In 1960, Peter Hall became director of the Royal Shakespeare Theatre, and set out to establish the nucleus of a permanent company working in both Stratford and London. One of his chief aims was that this company should explore the meaning of the texts. Actors were urged to place meaning above music in their delivery, directors and designers to be simpler and simpler, with as few scenic distractions from the text as possible. In all this, Hall was consciously reacting against the way of staging Shakespeare fashionable at the time, including by implication his own production of *Cymbeline*. By 1962 he had created the conditions which enabled William Gaskill's *Cymbeline* to achieve an overall clarity and consistency which had eluded his own version in 1957.

In a retrospect of the 1962 season published in the Royal Shakespeare Company's booklet *Crucial Years* (1963), the critic Roger Gellert wrote:

one now has a very clear picture of what to expect at Stratford, and to most of us it is a relief and a refreshment: light, air, space, the minimum of 'scenery'. Heavy, metallically gleaming objects are hung or planted in front of white screens, buff netting, or an uncluttered cyclorama. Furniture and clothes look lived-with, and texture is more sought-after than colour. (p. 8)

It was Gaskill's *Cymbeline*, in fact, that decisively established this style, and Gellert's description gives a good idea of Rene Allio's design. Upon entering the theatre, the audience was confronted with what Kenneth Tynan called a 'stage-scape of dazzling simplicity' (*Observer*, 22 July 1962). The entire stage, proscenium arch, and forestage were neutralised by being covered with off-white netting and backed by a white cyclorama. The effect was not only startling in itself, literally 'dazzling' to the eye; it was as far removed as it could possibly have been from Lila de Nobili's stage-filling set with its painted gauzes and its shifting chiaroscuro effects.

Bare staging is now very common for the presentation of Shakespeare, but it was an innovation in 1962. It established itself very quickly because it is likely to be a good starting point for a Shakespeare production, focusing attention on the actors, events, and language by avoiding distractions from them. That is the theory, at any rate. The method failed, in fact, with this very play on this same stage in 1979 because the director on that occasion seemed to have no intelligible view of the play to offer, or indeed any interesting way to use the acting area; instead of being liberated, the actors were dominated and dwarfed by the space: they simply came and went, established nothing, and so the play seemed pointless, thereby reinforcing the prejudice that it is in fact pointless.

At Stratford in 1962, however, the empty space was used very purposefully indeed. The actor who subsequently played one of Posthumus's jailers walked on to the bare stage and whistled. A group of Jacobean servants – the prompt-book called them 'zanies' – assembled. On further whistled cues, they gathered round the jailer and sat down; a large sculptured symbol featuring a rearing lion, which represented the British court, was flown in; and the doctor Cornelius arrived to tell the zanies the story so far, using the lines of the first gentleman to do so. In this way, as Mark Taylor's review in *Plays and Players* put it, 'the play [was] neatly framed' (October 1962). The zanies divided up the second gentleman's responses between them, expressing increasing incredulity:

'That a king's children should be so conveyed!', 'So slackly guarded!', 'And the search so slow / That could not trace them!' (I.i.64-6). By this simple framing device the apparent perversities and bizarre events that followed could be simply accepted as part of a tall story. And the zanies themselves played their part in its telling, enthusiastically entering into its spirit after their initial scepticism, and in the process adding an extra layer to the rich theatricality of the play.

They helped to bring on the simple pieces of furniture that suggested Britain or Rome, while above their heads further place-setting symbols were flown in and out as needed, notably a sculptured eagle for the Giacomo/Posthumus scenes: this neatly suggested Rome, and in preparing the audience for Jupiter's sub-sequent descent on his eagle, it also helped to minimise the incon-sistency between Giacomo's medieval Italy and Caius Lucius's classical one. The staging was a simple and economical way of moving swiftly between the various locations. Having initially lured the real audience into the play's own theatrical world by the use of a stage audience, the production used the zanies less and less, and technical means, especially flying and the revolve in the stage floor, more and more. During the first interval, before the first Welsh scene, a large but still simple cave was positioned on the back section of the revolve. It consisted of two upright slabs and a crosspiece, a little like Stonehenge in design; sometimes it stayed upstage, sometimes it came forward on the revolve, as for the first scene between Belarius and the princes, to bring the action as close to the audience as possible.

This principle was followed throughout the production, except where the full depth of the stage was exploited for large-scale effects such as the battle and the descent of Jupiter. T. C. Worsley described the result:

> Perhaps we don't at once, bounded as we are by our conventional view of what to expect from Shakespearian productions, immediately catch on. The first third, dodging between Ancient Bri-tain and Italy, is the least successful. We are still not quite with it. But once we reach Cambria and the outskirts of Milford Haven, and the old Morgan and his supposed sons come out from their cave . . . the trick works completely. (*Financial Times*, 18 July 1962)

The process described here attests to the unfailing effect of the Belarius/princes scenes, to the cumulative power of the play, and to the varying use of the cave, in different positions, as a strong unifying feature of the production.

Sometimes such brilliant theatrical devices are devised by directors to compensate for a supposedly weak play. But William Gaskill is not a director of that kind. In every production of his that I have seen, he has shown unfailing faith in his dramatist. He seems quite uninterested in imposing himself on his material, totally absorbed in the work he is presenting – which he stages as simply as possible, increasingly stripping away inessentials. Mark Taylor in *Plays and Players* began his review: 'Playwright led the way – 'She's wedded, / Her husband banished, she imprisoned': producer followed in his direct, straight to the point steps; and *Cymbeline* . . . shone forth astonishingly as the glory of the season.' 'Playwright led the way': this could be the motto of any Gaskill production. And the immediate advantage of this approach is that it places the play itself in the most favourable light. The dramatist's technique here appeared 'direct' and 'straight to the point', the much-criticised perversities were not concealed by being wrapped up. Quite the reverse: everything was mercilessly scrutinised. The play stood up well to such scrutiny. Perhaps it is not so bizarre and perverse after all. Gaskill has a particular gift for allowing a story to unfold, apparently, by itself, so that even the strangest events – for instance, the trunk, burial, and Jupiter scenes – seem to arise naturally out of the narrative. As Kenneth Tynan put it in his review, within the production's simplicity, 'events of extreme complexity are to unfold'.

Mark Taylor in his review agreed, and emphasised the crucial contribution of the designer, pointing out how the white set threw 'into sharp relief both carved, carpentered and quarried décor and subtly contrasted costumes (homespun Britain v. brocaded Italy). The olive and earth, ruby and gold contribution to this *Cymbeline* of designer Rene Allio . . . must not be under-estimated. Its highly sophisticated simplicity is the ideal foil for the play's complexities.' The basis of the costume style was medieval, taking its cue from Giacomo's suave, tight-fitting doublet in black and gold, with hanging sleeves; Posthumus shared the same fashion in sleeves, but made of rougher material, like that worn by the other Britons, and in their shades of brown and stone. Cymbeline was a medieval king in dull red robe with furred sleeves, the queen's wimpled head-dress was particularly medieval, and Cloten's fur-red doublet linked him visually to the king. The Romans had hints of classical armour, but the touches of gold, especially in Caius

Lucius's huge cloak, provided visual connections with Giacomo (and with Jupiter), while their heavy material meant that they did not depart too far from the basic rough medievalism.

Innogen began as a radiant, fair-haired medieval princess. Alan Brien caught the tone when he observed that 'unicorns would lay their horns in her lap' (*Sunday Telegraph*, 22 July 1962). She was later transformed into an equally radiant boy, when the image she presented, with her short fair hair and glowing face, gave her an uncanny resemblance to the figure of Flora in Botticelli's *Primavera*, where bold innocence subtly coexists with sensuous allure. The similarity did not extend to the clothes. As Fidele, she wore a simple homespun tunic, with leggings and sandals. Her brothers and Belarius wore rough doublets, trousers, and boots, trimmed with fur. There were touches of the primitive in these costumes, but again, they were entirely consistent with a medieval world. The clothes throughout were as successful as the set. They seemed comfortable for the actors and gave the impression of being well worn – 'clothes not costumes', to borrow Peter Hall's distinction from the pamphlet *Crucial Years*.

Much of this design, especially the well-worn costumes and the 'highly sophisticated simplicity', had a very specific theatrical origin. As Kenneth Tynan explained, Rene Allio came to Stratford 'from Roger Planchon's company in Lyons, where Brecht is the bible'. And earlier in 1962, Gaskill himself had directed a production of Brecht's *The Caucasian Chalk Circle* for the Royal Shakespeare Company in London. It was visually very similar to this *Cymbeline* with its white set and boldly simple props. The events were not so much acted as put on display. This was the famous, or notorious, Brechtian 'alienation' at work, by which actors are supposed to show their characters analytically, as if they were standing outside them, rather than impersonating them. In short, they display emotions rather than experiencing them, so that the audience too remains detached rather than being caught up in the events on stage. I take it that this is what literary critics mean when they claim that in *Cymbeline* Shakespeare is distancing the audience from the characters, their situations, and their emotions. This *Cymbeline*, therefore, provided a good test for the validity of this theory since, even more than John Barton's described in the first chapter, it placed the play within a frame which emphasised its theatricality, even its artifice. It was Brechtian in appearance; was it Brechtian in alienatory effect? It certainly had the effect of isolating and highlighting individual scenes or even speeches, of putting them on display and holding them up to scrutiny. But did this alienate audience response? This can only be answered by a detailed account of the performance as a whole.

Simple staging throws attention on to the text, but it also demands very strong performances that can dominate the bare stage and make the most of its opportunities. In addition, this play has an unusually large number of major roles. Gaskill had the strongest cast I have ever seen assembled for *Cymbeline*, and it was moreover a company that was used to working together as an ensemble: the advantages of Peter Hall's policies were very much in evidence. Nor was it an ensemble that required its members to suppress their individual personalities and talents: this was an ensemble of virtuosi. There was, throughout, a sense of actors relishing their craft, of enjoying the challenge of matching the play's virtuosity with their own. Gareth Lloyd Evans, in his *Guardian* review, said that Vanessa Redgrave (Innogen), Eric Porter (Giacomo) and Patrick Allen (Posthumus) were 'superb in speech and in timing', but added that 'their gaiety, gravity, pride and panache is cocooned in artificiality, and that the realities of grief, joy and venom are intermittent' (18 July 1962). He meant this as an adverse criticism, but it is more useful as an objective description, for it makes an important point about the play itself, the way in which those emotional realities are in a sense isolated, expressed in single moments, highlighted and spotlit. The production insisted upon an essential aspect of the play; and it is significant that Evans found the emotional realities intermittent, not absent.

The key performance in establishing the tone of the production was Eric Porter's Giacomo. The anonymous reviewer in *The Times*, catching this tone and taking the hint provided by the costume, wrote:

> Eric Porter's speaking of Giacomo's part was a delight. He, the betrayer of Innogen and Posthumus, was recognisable as a minor poet unable to resist the temptation to twist life into a neat little short story after the pattern of Boccaccio. His two victims, Vanessa Redgrave's Innogen and Patrick Allen's Posthumus, gained life at the beginning from the contrast they presented to the quick-witted schemer of Mr Porter's. (*The Times*, 18 July 1962)

This raises several important points about the part. First, this Giacomo was completely removed from tragedy; the issue simply didn't arise. Next, this performance made positively the point made negatively at Stratford in 1979; an Innogen and Posthumus depend very much on the actor of Giacomo to provide them with something to react to, and so to get their performances, and the play itself, off the ground. And the performance of Giacomo in turn depends crucially on the delivery of the text. The 'delight' of the *Times* reviewer was shared by most others, T. C. Worsley going so far as to speak of Eric Porter's 'customary perfection', so it is fortunate that Alan Brien offered a very specific description of what Porter's style was like: 'its fluid, unmannered, almost insolent, clarity and control of dramatic poetry, (is) always tuned to wring every last syllable of sense from the lines without once losing the rhythm' (*Sunday Telegraph*, 15 November 1964). The characteristics mentioned here indicate his approach to Giacomo, stylish and elegant rather than intense and tragic.

In Hall's production, Geoffrey Keen's Giacomo had provoked Posthumus with booming, glossy tones and a stagey manner which was not very helpful: the wager scene didn't seem to be about anything. Eric Porter was the opposite of all that: amused, ironic, watchful, taunting Posthumus not by attack but by subtle insinuation. Indeed, it was Posthumus who used the large physical and vocal gestures, very appropriate to a man with total confidence in himself and his wife – a dangerous confidence which this Giacomo was determined to take down a peg or two: 'I make my wager rather against your confidence than her reputation' (I.iv.108-9). The scene made complete sense. When Posthumus indignantly cried that Giacomo's attempt on Innogen would be met by 'a repulse', Porter simply laughed, and laughed again as he pointed out, casually and provocatively, that you cannot prevent ladies' flesh from tainting (I.iv.134). One moment summarised the whole scene: when Giacomo undertook to carry out the wager, Posthumus indignantly asked 'Will you?', outraged; there was a pause and Porter simply nodded casually, as if to say 'no problem', a response precisely calculated to take the wind, infuriatingly, out of Posthumus's sails.

Porter brought the same quick-witted, light-weight approach to his attempted seduction of Innogen, but here he was much more careful in his manipulative technique, and he took great care to establish plausibility throughout the scene. He delivered the convoluted speeches with such consummate ease that lines like

[48]

> Sluttery, to such neat excellence opposed,
> Should make desire vomit emptiness,
> Not so allured to feed (I.vi.45-7)

presented no problem at all. Their function was clear: they were intended to throw her off her guard and to create an atmosphere of obscure disgust and illicit sexuality by verbal innuendo:

> The cloyèd will,
> That satiate yet unsatisfied desire, that tub
> Both filled and running, ravening first the lamb,
> Longs after for the garbage. (I.vi.49-52)

Geoffrey Keen had ranted these speeches in Hall's production; in John Barton's they were cut. But what Mark Taylor called the 'stylised naturalism' of Porter's delivery made perfect sense of them: 'as the barbed and honeyed words of Giacomo flow from his mouth, they assume a fascinating offensiveness'. After the shift in the scene, when Giacomo gets rid of Pisanio, Porter adopted a different tack as he resumed his manoeuvres. The exchange between Innogen and himself was punctuated with insinuating pauses, and Innogen caught his manner as she began to doubt, with an ominous pause before 'My lord, I fear, / Has forgot Britain' (I.vi.113-14). Encouraged, he warmed to his theme, urging her to 'revenge', but he still refrained from overplaying his hand completely; as he dedicated himself to her sweet pleasure, he merely kissed her hand, before asking 'Let me my service tender on your *lips*' (I.vi.136-41); so when she called for Pisanio, it was easy for him to laugh and pretend that he was merely testing her. Since he had played the scene so lightly, so sophisticatedly, he was able to make this transition completely convincing, which is much harder in more heavyweight interpretations, as in the BBC television version, or at Stratford, Ontario in 1986, when Giacomo grabbed her crotch.

The sophistication both of the staging and of this performance ensured that the bedroom scene was the first big climax of the production. The bed was set on the upstage section of the revolve, and the trunk put into position, screened from the audience's view by one of the flown emblems at the front. As that flew out, the revolve brought the bed right round to the front of the stage, so that this crucial episode was played close to the audience. Like the other large pieces of furniture, the bed was very simple: carved wooden base, plain curtains, fur coverlet; Innogen got into bed wrapped in a sheet. As she lay down to sleep, there was a long pause, and the crickets mentioned in Giacomo's first line were audible. Very slowly the lid of the trunk opened, Porter stealthily emerged, and moved upstage of the bed to deliver the speech both to Innogen and to us: this meant that we felt its full impact while remaining aware of Innogen herself throughout.

This staging brought out the dual focus of the scene that Michael Taylor describes in his article 'The Pastoral Reckoning in *Cymbeline*':

> However innocent the lovers, we cannot help but see them as sexual objects designed to provoke the conspiracy of suggestiveness that gives them their ambivalent and attractive power. How much more attractive (and no less ambivalent) must be Innogen's appeal for us, when we hear not only from Giacomo how beautiful she is, but share with him in the actual vision of her loveliness, the naked extent of which will be determined only by the tact or bravado of the particular production in which she appears. (*Shakespeare Survey 36*, 1983, p. 103)

In this production Vanessa Redgrave was obviously naked beneath the sheet wrapped around her. She faced the audience during the first part of the soliloquy; at Giacomo's reference to 'th' madding of her lord' (II.ii.37), she stirred in her sleep and turned over, thus exposing her left breast and the mole upon it to Giacomo's view. Porter's immaculate eloquence and clarity then made the most of the cowslip comparison as of the whole speech. This staging threw attention upon the language and its suggestiveness, in both senses. Porter managed to suggest both Giacomo's sensitivity to her beauty, and the overtones of the voyeur, holding them in balance with an elegance and lightness of touch that seemed to me ideal.

The production brought out very clearly the irony that it is the apparent villain who expresses the greatest appreciation of Innogen, and her husband who tries to kill her. Patrick Allen began with a great advantage as Posthumus. Unlike Richard Johnson in Hall's production, he did not look like a conventional romantic hero – his features are somewhat battered – and he was rather older than usual: he was certainly no *jeune premier*. So he could not rely on a romantic appearance, as Johnson had done. He had to act the part, to explore it and to express his findings through his delivery of the language. The angry soliloquy of II.v. was the key to the performance. It was prepared for by the careful timing of the preceding scene, and particularly by the use of further strategic pauses, establishing a nervous tension between Posthumus and Giacomo, as in the Giacomo/Innogen scene, with Eric Porter once again manipulating the pauses to suggestive effect: '*(pause)* Your lady *(pause)* is / One of the fair'st . . .' (II.iv.31-2). There was a further longish pause for Posthumus to read Innogen's letter, perhaps also to suggest a touch of insecurity that was then dispelled by the confident relief of 'All is well yet' (II.iv.39). Giacomo played Posthumus skilfully, relishing the description of the bedroom; Posthumus laughed confidently on 'This is her honour!'(II.iv.91), whereupon Giacomo pricked the bubble of that confidence by coolly handing him the bracelet. The soliloquy emerged as the natural response of a man whose confident pride had been wounded. Even so, Patrick Allen's delivery of it came as a shock. Instead of the quasi-tragic rant of, for example, Richard Johnson, he delivered it with an outraged indignation that suggested humiliation rather than heart-break. It was very easy to accommodate the conventional cynicism and misogyny within this interpretation, and the entire speech held together. But it was so startling that I vividly remember thinking 'He'll never get away with this; what about the instruction to kill Innogen?' – yet at the same time thinking that the delivery fitted the speech exactly. It caught precisely the tone of 'overwrought heroic folly', to use G. K. Hunter's felicitous description of the style (new Arden *All's Well That Ends Well*, 1959, p. lvi). Nor was there in fact any problem later: this Posthumus was just the kind of man who would rashly instruct Pisanio to kill Innogen, and then as quickly repent his folly before discovering she was innocent. And in making the soliloquy outraged and indignant rather than quasi-tragic, Allen also made the rhetoric of the final lines sound rather hollow, as if Posthumus did not wholly believe in his attack on her – and that, too, helped to motivate his later repentance. This character is not a *chevalier sans peur et sans reproche*, and when played so the part makes no sense, because the interpretation does not reconcile everything that Posthumus says and does. This performance did.

If this production demonstrated how Shakespeare has complicated the ostensible romantic hero, it also revealed the complexities of his rival. Here, Gaskill developed the excellent work begun in Hall's version, and much of my account of Clive Revill's Cloten applies to Clive Swift's as well. There was exceptional critical unanimity about this performance. Reviewer after reviewer singled out Swift's Cloten alongside Eric Porter's Giacomo and Vanessa Redgrave's Innogen for special praise. Robert Muller summarised the range of the performance: 'a brilliant portrait . . . combining vanity, obtuseness and explosive hysteria (*Daily Mail*, 18 July 1962). The *Times* reviewer added detail: 'This was a complete portrait of a man who, if he did not have a screw loose, might have been a forceful character, but who actually is, as he partly suspects, a butt and a misfit.' Clive Swift gave this impression through a mannerism of drawing himself upright, with his head held stiffly back and slightly to one side, as he tried to follow points that were being made but always just failed to do so. Swift's naturally slow, very deliberate style of speaking, combined with the pauses that were much used in this production, gave the impression of a man who was slow on the uptake but was trying very hard to work out ideas partly forming in his mind: 'Here's my purse. (*Pause, as an idea began*:) Hast (*pause*) any of thy late master's (*pause, to emphasise that the idea had formed*:) garments in thy possession?' (III.v.123-4) The vanity was expressed in emphatic statements like 'I *mean*, the lines of my body are as well drawn as his' (IV.i.8-9) and in the violent recoil when Innogen told him, with all Vanessa Redgrave's startling candour, 'I care not for you' (II.iii.105), the hysteria by outbursts of shouting and stamping, as in his denunciation of Posthumus as 'a base slave, / A hilding for a livery, a squire's cloth, / A pantler – not so eminent' (II.iii.119-21). The only drawback of this performance was that Clive Swift is totally different from Patrick Allen verbally, temperamentally, and especially physically, so that the connections between the two characters could not be made. This should have raised problems when Innogen came to identify the parts of Cloten's corpse so positively with Posthumus's, but it didn't seem to. No reviewer remarked on the problem, and the point probably is that there are so many other demands on the audience (not to mention the actress) in this episode that one responds to Innogen's emotional crisis rather than to its immediate cause.

The production's handling of that scene, however, needs to be considered in the context of the presentation of Belarius and the princes. After the skills of Eric Porter and Patrick Allen had launched the wager plot and with it the play, the arrival of this group consolidated the production's grip. Indeed, T. C. Worsley thought that it was with their arrival that the production's technique took complete hold on the audience. As the revolve spun round, bringing the cave from the back to the front of the stage, Belarius and the boys emerged on to the apron and saluted the heavens – a simple ritual at once far-away-and-long-ago and touch-ingly real. The princes carried bows, with which they later threatened Innogen when she intruded into their domain. Paul Hardwick's rich, dark-hued voice was used very flexibly to suggest Belarius's integrity, warmth, and goodness and, in an entirely unsentimental way, his piety as well. He gave full value to his account of his rural world,

> Where I have lived at honest freedom, paid
> More pious debts to heaven than in all
> The fore-end of my time. (III.iii.71-3)

These beautiful lines are usually omitted on the entirely misguided grounds that Belarius is an unconvincing puppet who cannot be allowed to talk for too long. That claim was once again swiftly disproved in Belarius's soliloquy, as Paul Hardwick simply turned to the audience and told them his story – though it was, admittedly, particularly easy to do so in the theatrically overt circumstances of this production.

What was perhaps less easy to communicate in those circum-stances was the ubiquitous rural imagery of these scenes, since the design did not harmonise with such language as the oaks, ivy, and hanging woods of Hall's version had done. Barry MacGregor and Brian Murray nevertheless vividly conveyed the human emo-tions that this language expresses, especially the princes' love for Innogen and their welcoming of her: 'The night to th' owl and morn to th' lark less welcome' (III.vi.91). There was a mixture of instinctive tenderness and humour in the exchanges between brothers and sister, with much physical contact. Guiderius touched 'Fidele' in comradely, jokey fashion at 'Were you a woman, youth', and broke up the next line with embarrassed pauses at the dawning of a new and unfamiliar emotion: 'I should woo hard', he began, then, feeling that this didn't seem quite the right thing to say, he broke off and tried again: 'but be your groom (*pause*) – in honesty' (III.vi.66-7). In its stumbling awkwardness, it was both funny and touching, and the scenes were lit up by many such moments. When Guiderius returned to the stage with Cloten's severed head, he held it behind his back with a mixture of bravado, itching to show what he had done, and apprehension as to what Belarius's reaction might be. T. C. Worsley commented: 'We can smile at the triumphant boy bringing in Cloten's head; for we can in fact now move easily between laughter and tears.' And he added that 'we can accept on these terms Innogen's waking with a headless trunk in her arms, because we can both smile at the excess and be persuaded by the grief of Vanessa Redgrave's winningly genuine Innogen'.

That episode began with another prolonged pause to emphasise Arviragus's entry from the cave with Innogen in his arms. The moment was more charged with emotion even than usual, with Arviragus in tears as he tenderly laid her on the floor, so that Guiderius had to comfort him with 'Why, he but sleeps' (IV.ii.216). The flower-speech and the dirge arose naturally out of the situation, without any hint of set pieces. After the mingled sweetness and sadness of the ritual burial, Gaskill prolonged the stillness with what the prompt-book called an 'inordinately long pause'. This pause ensured that the audience fully experienced the sense of a death and ceremonial burial, and it obviously intensified the focus on Innogen in an extremely bold way which typified the handling of what followed. The staging was bold, but it was also careful to make each moment as plausible as possible. John Russell Brown's account in *Shakespeare Survey 16* makes this clear:

> the audience was held in rapt belief and concern as Innogen was roused from her drugged sleep to feel [Cloten's body] at her side. Miss Redgrave carried this scene by boldly accepting the improbability of her half-conscious thoughts; even as she said
>> it is
>> Without me, as within me: not imagined, felt
> she was still half unconvinced. She touched the stuffed and painted canvas which represented the bloody neck and said 'A headless man!' as a quiet, flat recognition, such as comes before full realization. She did not gain a fully responsive consciousness until she cried 'Murder in heaven?'

Production and performance took great care to lure the audience into accepting and believing in the scene, and it clearly succeeded in winning their 'belief' and 'concern'. Brown continues:

> The other major difficulty of the soliloquy:
>> Where is thy head? where's that? Ay me! where's that?
>> Pisanio might have killed thee at the heart
>> And left this head on
> was met with comparable clarity, for the question which sounds absurd in considered or temperate speech was spoken in full flight of passion, and gave to that expression of feeling the recklessness and directness of imagination, and of thought which is too rapid and instinctive to be sensible. (pp. 150-1)

While this interpretation sought to make the speech as convincing as possible, it also brought out the way in which the first part of it hovers between sleep and waking, so that Innogen feels that she must be dreaming, and that what she then experiences is a kind of waking nightmare – a point of which subsequent productions made a great deal. When at the end of the speech she hugged the corpse, she covered herself with blood. I think that this is what the phrase 'Give colour to my pale cheek with thy blood' (IV.ii.332) suggests, rather than that she dips her hands into the severed neck and daubs her face with the blood, as in the BBC television version and in the Oxford Shakespeare's stage direction. The daubing seems pointless, an extraneous baroque flourish, whereas Innogen's blooding through embracing the corpse at least has an obvious cause; and the sense that this production made of every scene should give us pause before dismissing anything in the play as wanton display. Brown's point that the audience was held in 'rapt belief and concern' is borne out by other reviewers, *The Times* remarking that Vanessa Redgrave's 'uncompromising playing of the scene . . . was utterly satisfying in its truthfulness'. Stanley Wells has, privately, added his vivid impression of the scene: 'I thought it was important that when Cloten's body was carried in, its horror was not stylised: the veins were dangling from the neck where the head had been. The simultaneity of horror and beauty in this scene matched the play's fusion of extremes of emotion.'

The episode between Innogen and Caius Lucius which ends the scene is frequently cut to ribbons in performance but here was played almost in full and given its proper value, which is considerable. Brown describes it in detail:

> Innogen's reawaking to hear Lucius questioning her was similarly affecting by a simple and convinced performance. She gazed at him unmoving while he slowly asked:
>> What's thy interest
> In this sad wreck? How came it? Who is it?
> What art thou?
> and without changing this impression of inward involvement she then spoke slowly, one broken word at a time: 'I am nothing'. Only by telling her story did she seem to gain a full knowledge of what she was speaking. Miss Redgrave's performance in this scene was judged by an artistic sense that responded to both the fantasy and pathos as manifestations of a mind overmastered by feeling, and it had the strength and simplicity to carry conviction in every change of consciousness. (p. 151)

This account draws attention to the tempo and function of this passage: slow, steady, awakening from the nightmare. Shakespeare is providing a transition from the violent intensity of the soliloquy, and only very gradually bringing Innogen to the point where she is able to put her horrific experience behind her and begin a new life as Caius Lucius's page.

To abbreviate the passage sacrifices all this; and it reduces, as most productions do, Caius Lucius's contribution to the scene and to the play in general. As the Roman ambassador, he is a figure of administrative authority, but throughout the play he tempers sternness with humaneness and courtesy. No sooner has he declared war on Cymbeline on Augustus Caesar's behalf, for instance, than he instantly adds: 'Thus defied, / I thank thee for myself', and draws from Cymbeline a corresponding courtesy which the king shows rarely elsewhere: 'Thou art welcome, Caius' (III.i.67-8). This blending of authority with humanity is something that Shakespeare often presents in his rulers, including Theseus in *A Midsummer Night's Dream* and the Duke in *The Comedy of Errors*, who both ultimately modify the sternness of a harsh law when to do so will promote the happiness of their subjects. Tony Steedman made much of all three parts at Stratford in 1962, simply by bringing to each a quiet, unassertive authority touched with courtesy and generosity. Caius Lucius is, in little, an example of the magnanimity of the true statesman, and part of the point is that he embodies precisely what Cymbeline lacks, or has forgotten. That is why the role should never be reduced, either by cuts or under-casting. And Shakespeare's manipulation of the plot so that Caius Lucius arrives at the lowest moment of Innogen's fortunes is not an example of dramatic over-ingenuity: it provides the humanity and kindness which is just what she needs at this point.

Tony Steedman beautifully achieved all this; but when, at the end of the scene, he urged Innogen to 'be cheerful', he got a laugh. It was not unkind laughter, merely the response of the audience to the distance between Innogen's extreme situation and the possibility of cheerfulness. It was also the release of tension pent up for so long in the audience as well as on the stage. In this instance, in fact, laughter was evidence of the powerful hold the scene had upon the audience, rather than the reverse. Several critics mentioned this point, for example Mark Taylor: 'Somehow we can laugh, a little squeamishly . . . while, at the same time, opening our hearts to so bereaved, so lovely' an Innogen. Such 'squeamish' laughter can act as a kind of safety-valve for the audience's emotions; the theatrical virtuosity of the production enabled the audience, as T. C. Worsley put it, to 'move easily between laughter and tears'. This could be a description of how audiences respond to Shakespearian comedy in performance, and is a useful reminder that in *Cymbeline* Shakespeare pushes his earlier comic technique to extremes: Innogen goes through the harshest experiences so that her reunion with her husband may be the happier and more valued an experience. As Caius Lucius puts it at this point, 'Some falls are means the happier to arise' (IV.ii.404).

As with Innogen, so with Posthumus, in the battle and Jupiter scenes, for which Gaskill reserved his greatest *coups de théâtre*. The battle was played around the two rocks of Belarius's cave; the two uprights were separated and re-set at the back of the revolve to create the 'narrow lane' in which the battle takes place, and the crosspiece which had formed the roof of the cave now jutted out to provide a spur on which Posthumus could stand to dominate the field. The battle itself was brilliantly stylised, at once an elaborate theatrical showpiece and a piece of storytelling which corresponded in every particular to the stage directions to Posthumus's subsequent account of what happened.

The Folio directions specify that the two armies enter, 'march over, and go out'. Gaskill took this bald phrase as the cue for a precisely-drilled series of marches and countermarches by the British army, led by Cymbeline and Pisanio, and the Roman one, led by Caius Lucius, around the revolve and the rock-cave. The battle was accompanied by music, but its use was functional rather than atmospheric. A gong and timpani clashes cued the various military manoeuvres, and they varied in speed to accentuate the fluctuating fortunes of the two armies. They got faster and faster as the Britons were routed, then slowed down as Posthumus, Belarius, and the princes turned the rout into victory. The armies froze as Posthumus and Giacomo fought their duel, and for Giacomo's soliloquy, then resumed afterwards, exactly as the Folio specifies: 'the battle continues'. The British army was routed at the back of the stage, and fled downstage between the rocks of the cave which now constituted the narrow lane. Cymbeline was captured at the front of the stage, whereupon the revolve spun round, bringing Posthumus, Belarius, and the princes forward, standing on the rocks: the 'narrow lane' was now near the front of the stage. Caius Lucius and the Romans attacked the British quartet, but the four of them defeated waves of Roman soldiers, and then rescued Cymbeline at the front. The British soldiers who had been routed now revived and pursued the Romans upstage, through the 'lane', as Posthumus's account specifies (V.v.43-51). Belarius returned Cymbeline his sword and the Britons marched off in triumph. The whole elaborate manoeuvre was carried off with the utmost dash and theatrical expertise, and was greeted with applause.

The only danger with this virtuoso battle was that it might have upstaged the Jupiter scene. In fact, it prepared the audience for it. The two jailers brought a large cage on stage, and locked Posthumus inside it. One of them whistled (as he had done to start the play) for a line to be dropped from the flies, which was attached to the roof of the cage. Posthumus delivered his soliloquy inside the cage which was then hoisted off the ground. There was another long pause, as there had been before Giacomo's emergence from the trunk and before Innogen's awakening by the body, which served to link the three episodes together. As Posthumus's dream began, the revolve slowly started to move and, in a hazy half-light, the ghosts of Posthumus's family moved slowly, in a series of turns, against the motion of the revolve, an aptly weird physical accompaniment to their bizarre speeches. In this way, as the Folio direction puts it, 'They circle Posthumus round as he lies sleeping.' Then came the sensation of the production. The revolve stopped; exactly as the Folio prescribes, there was a thunderclap, the ghosts fell on their knees, and Jupiter descended. There were no half-measures. The wing-span of the huge copper eagle was about a third of the width of the stage. Jupiter wore a simple gold costume and make-up, and supported himself by holding the solid steel pole upon which the eagle was suspended; and he was spotlit in golden light. John Corvin delivered his lines firmly and clearly and returned to the heavens, the ghosts vanished, the cage was lowered to the floor, and the arrival of the jailers to unhook the cage brought the dream world abruptly back to earth.

This was easily the most striking staging of this scene in my experience, and it was achieved so simply, with entirely modern technical means, that there seems no excuse whatever to dodge or muff Jupiter's descent, as at Stratford in 1957, 1979, and 1987, or on television, where it would have been particularly easy to achieve with superimposed images. But after this triumphant success, Gaskill oddly omitted Jupiter's prophecy and therefore all reference to it, the only major cut in the production. It was very hard to see why. This cut of course deprived Posthumus of his comments upon the prophecy, and the parallel he draws between its strangeness and the events of his own life was particularly missed in a production which was so successful in making strange events seem a believable part of the characters' lives. Without the prophecy, the descent of Jupiter provides a simple promise of present suffering giving way to future happiness, repeating the hope offered to Innogen by Caius Lucius earlier:

> He shall be lord of lady Innogen,
> And happier much by his affliction made. (V.v.201-2)

'Even that last scene', wrote T. C. Worsley, 'that we always thought impossible to stage succeeds under this treatment.' Cymbeline's throne, a simple carved seat with a plain silver back, was placed in front of a large tent-like canopy which blocked off most of the main stage and concentrated all the action at the front of the stage for the multiple discoveries. The company played it with great gusto, presenting it, as they had the whole play, for all 'it is worth at any given moment in humour, pathos and spectacle' (Roger Gellert, *New Statesman*, 27 July 1962). And here Tom Fleming's testy Cymbeline came into his own as he attempted to follow the numerous revelations and coincidences. He was particularly sorely tried by Giacomo's convoluted narrative, even though it was considerably shortened, as he repeatedly tried to get a word in edgeways. Patrick Allen played Posthumus's outcry as he had done the angry soliloquy, with large vocal and physical gestures. Phrases like 'The temple / Of virtue was she; yea, and she herself' (V.vi.221-2) came over not so much as examples of over-writing as of Posthumus's own rashness and impulsiveness. He moved constantly up and down the stage, so that Vanessa Redgrave had to force herself upon him to gain a hearing; in his frenzy, he violently dashed her to the ground. This flamboyant performance served to support the Folio reading of Innogen's next speech:

> Think that you are upon a rock, and now
> Throw me again. (V.vi.263-4)

The emendation of 'rock' to 'lock' adopted by many editions, including the Oxford Shakespeare, on the grounds that Innogen is comparing her embrace to a wrestling grip, a 'lock', has always seemed to me far-fetched, and this context suggested that it is in fact unnecessary: with Posthumus using the large-scale gestures suggested by his speeches, it was perfectly comprehensible that Innogen should compare him to man standing upon a rock, about to hurl her into the sea. It somehow added to the moving quality of his famous reply:

> Hang there like fruit, my soul,
> Till the tree die. (V.vi.264-5).

The pace was fast and furious after this, humour jostling with pathos as the action moved between the forthrightness of Guiderius's

> I cut off's head,
> And am right glad he is not standing here
> To tell this tale of mine. (V.vi.297-9)

and the tenderness of Belarius's blessing of his 'sons'. It was in writing about this production that the *Times* review I quoted in the first chapter found that 'the most beautiful thing of all in the play' seemed to be the relationship between Belarius and the princes. The reviewer continued:

> and this was, after all, a relationship founded on a fiction. Belarius was not the father of the two young men. Yet this, an elective affinity as one might call it, had worked out well, whereas most of the other situations in the play – those between parent and child, husband and wife, lover and beloved – had involved the characters in near ruin. (*The Times*, 18 July 1962)

Near, but not complete, ruin: the review usefully brings out how in performance the Belarius/princes relationship balances the Innogen/Posthumus one. In this production the balance was perfectly maintained, and emphasised in this final scene. When Cymbeline said to Innogen, 'Thou hast lost by this a kingdom', Vanessa Redgrave replied with all her frank, open radiance 'No, my lord, / I have got two worlds by 't' (V.vi.375-6), embracing her brothers with one arm and her husband with the other. Overwhelmed by a mixture of emotion and bewilderment, Tom Fleming's Cymbeline threw up his arms and extended his forgiveness to the Romans – 'Let them be joyful too!' – to the delighted, sympathetic laughter of the audience. This scene conclusively made the point that laughter need not distance the audience from the events on stage. Here everyone in the theatre was quite clearly caught up in the joy, forgiveness and reunion which the overt theatricality was presenting.

Critical response to this *Cymbeline* was almost unanimously enthusiastic. Even Robert Muller, who had gone with low expectations of the play, was completely won over by the staging: 'I had never hoped to be so beguiled and thrilled', he wrote, 'but in William Gaskill's triumphant production just about everything works.' And he made the further point that the individual achievement derived from a more general one: 'Everything to which the Royal Shakespeare Company has aspired in its three years under Peter Hall's direction was fulfilled ... in a production which glistened with the bloom of greatness' (*Daily Mail*, 18 July 1962). So if Peter Hall did not entirely bring off *Cymbeline* in 1957, he created the conditions for Gaskill to do so in 1962. Alan Brien made another important point: 'We begin to realise with what subtle expertise Shakespeare has written these roles and their interchanges with each other' (*Sunday Telegraph*, 22 July 1962). Gaskill's greatest achievement was to reveal the quality of the play itself. The theatrical virtuosity (what Gareth Lloyd Evans in the *Guardian* called the production's 'theatrical largesse') did not inhibit the actors but liberated them to express the extremes of grief, love, joy, and so on. The audience was not only delighted but moved and involved as well. T. C. Worsley concluded that Gaskill's approach 'solves so many of the technical problems of staging *Cymbeline* that it is bound to be a prototype on which future directors will work'. This turned out not to be the case, and the other productions discussed here represent very different approaches to the play, all of them interesting, none of them quite so successful.

CHAPTER IV

'The neuroticism of tragedy': Elijah Moshinsky's BBC television version, 1982

To move from the theatrical sophistication and technical expertise of William Gaskill's production to Elijah Moshinsky's for the BBC television Shakespeare is to enter a different world. In 1980 Moshinsky directed *All's Well That Ends Well* for the television series. In its intimacy and realism, *All's Well* is especially suited to television treatment. Moshinsky's early seventeenth-century costumes and interiors, based on paintings by Rembrandt and Vermeer, worked well: Jacobean rooms have the advantage on television that they communicate a 'lived-in' quality, Jacobean clothes that they do not draw undue attention to themselves as 'costumes'. Together with the frequent use of close-up which television encourages, they invite the viewer to concentrate less on externals than on what the characters are saying and feeling and even thinking, by presenting the face motionless while 'voice-over' communicates the thought process. Moshinsky set *Cymbeline* in the same period, though he was aiming at a quite different effect from the realistic society he had established in *All's Well*.

Rembrandt was again the starting point: the portrait of Agatha Bass was, apparently, the inspiration for the image of a Jacobean princess that Helen Mirren presents as Innogen, 'quite severe and yet young and quite princess-like' (BBC edition, p. 18). There is one superb visual effect in the production when, at the start of I.vi, the camera moves slowly across a Jacobean long gallery illumi-

[62]

nated by tall windows towards Innogen's solitary figure sitting absolutely motionless, lost in thought. The shot perfectly captures her sense of isolation at a court ruled by 'a father cruel and a stepdame false' and separated from her banished husband (I.vi.1-3). The sense of stillness is prolonged because, as the camera nears her face, it reveals that this too is motionless: the lines are spoken in 'voice-over', and accompanied by a broad cello melody, to romantic effect. Here the Jacobean setting perfectly catches the mood of the heroine, though it does not always have such evocative potential. The action takes place in a series of Jacobean interiors, with tapestries on the walls, sparely dignified chairs and tables, a globe, and fires crackling in John Smythson fireplaces. This is very much indoor Shakespeare. Cymbeline wears a rust over-robe with a huge black fur collar, the Queen is a Catherine de Medici figure dressed with sombre restraint and a total lack of exaggeration, in keeping with Claire Bloom's restrained performance. The rest are dressed in sober Jacobean splendour; Giacomo's black leather travelling outfit is particularly stylish. The designers found Rembrandt useful as a reference because he uses 'not only real people but allegorical figures too, which is useful for classical reference' (p. 19). But so far as I can see, they didn't use him for that purpose: the Romans wear breastplates over shirts or doublets, and Jupiter is the most soberly-clad Jacobean gentleman in the show.

Exterior scenes in the studio always make television designers anxious, and the Welsh scenes are extremely stylised. The landscape is covered by snow, made out of a plastic insulating material, and dotted with a few stark silver birches . It is also lit in a weird reddish glow, a surreal rather than a realistic landscape, and it contrasts markedly with the realistic idiom established by the interiors. This emphasises a central split in the production between the style adopted for the 'main' plot and that adopted for the princes plot. One of the more effective consequences of this split is the treatment of Innogen herself. As Moshinsky himself puts it in the BBC edition, 'Innogen is exactly like a woman of her period at the beginning, a Jacobean character, and at the end is a much more modern boy' (p. 18), despite wearing a Jacobean doublet rather too big for her.

This split is part of Moshinsky's concern to parallel by visual means the characters' 'duplicitous' natures. He sees this two-facedness as an aspect of the play's concern with moral ambiguity:

'Pisanio . . . is the symbol of that moral ambiguity because no-one knows whether he's good or bad. The queen, for example, says about him that he's a 'sly and constant knave' – he's both sly *and* constant' (p. 17). This is to make undue fuss about ambiguity. Pisanio is a straightforward character, an honest man who uses 'slyness' to protect his mistress and his master's interests in an environment where both are endangered – especially by the Queen, who is no reliable witness about his moral qualities. This forced interpretation is a consequence of Moshinsky's attempt to push the play towards a kind of moral ambiguity it does not possess.

The opening scene gives a good idea of the production style and of the television techniques employed. Cymbeline sits brooding beside a fire during the opening conversation, which is very low-key and has to compete with loud incidental music, which is over-insistent throughout the play. The lines

> We must forbear. Here comes the gentleman,
> The Queen and Princess

are omitted, understandably in a filmed version, and there is a filmic cut to the Queen's emphatic 'No!' in the next line. But although it is understandable, the jump is very abrupt; it fails to provide a substitute, in televison terms, for the simple transition from one part of the scene to another which the omitted lines provide. A small point here becomes a very large problem indeed later on. Moshinsky cuts from the end of one scene (often *before* the end) to the start of the next without even a token break, for instance a short fade, such as is regularly used in television plays. The transition I have already mentioned from the Queen in I.v. across the long gallery to Innogen in I.vi. is the exception that proves the rule. Otherwise, anyone who did not know the play would surely be very confused by these arbitrary jumps, and when in Act IV Moshinsky starts chopping the scenes into small fragments and intercuts between scenes with no hint of transition or explanation, anyone new to the play would become very confused. To this problem I must return.

Helen Mirren muffs Innogen's very first line: 'O dissembling courtesies!' she cries, instead of 'courtesy' (I.i. 85). Does it matter? Perhaps not very much here, but it happens a great deal, much more seriously, in later scenes. It indicates a lack of concern for what Shakespeare has written, and it underlines the slipshod, hastily-thrown-together look and sound of the televison series.

Cymbeline was recorded in a week, which seems to me an absurdly short time for a complex Shakespeare play. These considerations may not seem to have much relevance to the question of interpretation, but a major difficulty is that the interpretation seems confused partly because the execution is so messy, presumably because there was no time for re-takes to be made. Mirren's imprecision is the more noticeable by contrast with the superb clarity and edge of Claire Bloom's Medici Queen Mother, marvellously watchful, utterly free from caricature, but suddenly revealing bared fangs as she says to Innogen 'Fie! *you* must give way' (I.i.159). It is a flash of steely Medici authority, though I think the alternative reading, that the Queen speaks the line hypocritically to Cymbeline in order to give Innogen the impression that she is on her side, makes better sense – and would have fitted even better with the image of Medici cunning. But Claire Bloom's detailed, accurate performance is a model of how to transfer a theatrical role to the television screen.

Largely through this performance of the Queen, but also of course through the designs, a seventeenth-century court world is conjured up in such detail as to suggest that Moshinsky might have been aiming for a production which brought out the possible connection between Cymbeline and James I. A glance at Richard Johnson's caricatured, ranting Cymbeline makes that seem unlikely; and it turns out that all the detailed Jacobean realism has no specifically Jacobean significance at all. It is just a way of suggesting a roughly 'Shakespearian' ambiance, a neutral starting-point for an interpretation that has nothing to do with the world of James I. Moshinsky is specific about that: 'It's the opposite of *All's Well*. In *All's Well* I felt I had to make it social, realistic, because of the social levels in conflict in that society. Here I've got the realism to mean something else, it's nightmare realism' (p. 17). He needs to do this because of his uncompromisingly sombre view of the play: 'it's a very dark play, it deals with evil at great depth'. Moreover, and this is the key to his production, 'it's a tragedy, and what stops it from being a tragedy where everyone dies is the intervention of the gods ... and it's to be performed ... with all the intensity and neuroticism of a tragedy' (p. 17).

So Moshinsky is interested in neuroticism, psychology, what is going on inside people's minds – and even what is going on in their dreams – and the technique of his television production is devised to support this interest. As I noted earlier, he argues that there are two levels of action in the trunk, burial, and Jupiter scenes, an objective and subjective level. The subjective level 'is like a series of nightmares', and television, he claims, gives him the chance to make the trunk scene, for instance, like 'a nightmare about the presence of Giacomo which we know, objectively, to be true'. What then does Moshinsky make of a tragic, neurotic, psychological approach?

The first thing to say is that the two wager scenes between Giacomo and Posthumus work well on television, given the basic 'tragic' approach, which demands a golden hero falling victim to a lip-curling Italianate villain. The intimacy, detailed realism, and close-up of television are ideal for the tension of these scenes. The first of them takes place at a table – Moshinsky always seats his characters at tables whenever possible since this helps to focus the groupings tightly for the television camera – with Giacomo and Posthumus playing chess, which of course intensifies the sense of the two of them attempting to out-manoeuvre one another. The tension, the quiet, almost whispered exchanges, the close focus on the two faces over the chessboard – all this makes the setting-up of the wager very exciting indeed. Posthumus is calm, mature, thoughtful, not easily provoked, so Giacomo has to do all the work, which he does by mannerisms and insinuations. A sceptical 'ummm' precedes 'You may wear her in title yours; but, you know, strange fowl light upon neighbouring ponds' (I.iv. 86-7), and Posthumus edges his remark 'I do nothing doubt you have store of thieves' (I.iv.94-5) in response; the bridling tone motivates Filario's intervention. But still this Posthumus is slow to explode; when he does, however, in reaction to Giacomo's curt 'You are afraid', the sensible emendation of the Folio's 'You are a friend' (I.iv. 132), he tosses the ring onto the chessboard with a clatter at 'I *dare* you to this match' (I.iv.143), and Giacomo obscenely balances the ring on the tip of his finger as he talks about enjoying 'the dearest bodily part of your mistress' (I.iv.147-8).

The second scene between them is equally effective, again set at a table. And again Posthumus burns on a very slow fuse, in marked contrast to Patrick Allen's rash and volatile rendering in Gaskill's version. 'Sparkles this stone as it was wont?' (II.iv.40) is smilingly confident; 'If you can make't apparent / That you have (*slight pause of distaste*:) tasted her in bed' (II.iv.56–7) is very steady, considering the subject matter, almost reducing it to a scientific or mathematical proof to be demonstrated clinically, without any emotional involvement; the terse 'proceed' is delivered in the same cool tone. Best, and most confident of all, is the calmly ironic 'This is her honour?' (II.iv.91) after Giacomo has described the bedroom, and it makes the greatest possible contrast with the actual explosion when it comes. Giacomo slyly gives Posthumus a brief glimpse of the bracelet on his wrist and then quickly covers it again with his glove; Posthumus's hand slams down on Giacomo's wrist – 'Jove!' – to get another glimpse of it. When he attempts to recover, with the suggestion that Innogen may have sent it to him, Giacomo's cool, factual question 'She writes so to you, doth she?' (II.iv.105) is much more challenging than a more taunting delivery. And instead of the customary furious outburst on 'Oh, no, no, no', this Posthumus takes the challenge seriously: very slowly, reluctantly, he picks up the letter and glances through it: 'no', grimly; 'no', still reading; then the outburst comes: 'no, 'tis true!' Once convinced, a new Posthumus emerges. The snarling starts, his face distorts and his lip trembles as he delivers the word 'w-w-whore' (II.iv.128), so that Filario's plea for patience is sorely needed. This Posthumus's imagination takes on the obscene suggestiveness of this Giacomo.

The ensuing soliloquy is spat out with unrelenting tragic intensity in a lurid red light, the camera close in upon his face. The twisted grimace and bared teeth bring a horrible sneer to 'a pudency so rosy' (II.v.11), and he gets all the grossness of 'Cried "Uuuh!" and *mounted*' (II.v.17). Michael Pennington is far too intelligent to skate over such phrases in generalised rant, as Richard Johnson did in Hall's production, but nevertheless all this detail is set within a framework of undeviating tragic intensity, so that the final effect is monotonous, and lacks variety. His tragic collapse, Othello-like, from calm, confident trust to gross, shattered disintegration is so total that it is going to be extremely hard to make the transition to Posthumus's forgiveness of Innogen before he knows her to be innocent. This Posthumus would have been incapable of such a thing, as the production seems to acknowledge by giving him a totally different personality when he reappears. The fact that it was necessary to do this demonstrates that Tillyard's analysis of this speech cited in the first chapter gets things completely the wrong way round. It is in fact tragic intensity which is the 'worst possible preparation' for Posthumus's subsequent repentance whereas, as Patrick Allen showed, it is perfectly possible to move from the cynicism and hollow rhetoric to the repentance, since the modulations at the end of the speech suggest something insecure and unconvinced about Posthumus's intensity. Shakespeare knows what he is about, if only his interpreters would take the trouble to find out what that is, instead of imposing a generalised concept (like 'tragedy') upon the speech, thus ironing out its details.

A strange feature of this speech calls for comment. Like all the soliloquies in the play, it is delivered not to the camera, but slightly away from it, at an angle. Moshinsky's motive for this is to provide 'menacing perspectives' in keeping with his dark, tragic approach. But the effect is that the actor and/or the character is evading the viewers, rather than communicating with them, which is the purpose of a soliloquy. I would have thought that of all theatrical conventions, soliloquy is the easiest to transfer to television, for there is a direct parallel between talking to a theatre audience and, via the camera, to the viewer. We are used to people addressing us directly on television, and exactly how well this can be turned to advantage in Shakespeare is demonstrated by Anthony Quayle's playing to the camera in the BBC *Henry IV* plays. There is of course a difference between Falstaff's button-holing manner and Posthumus's 'overwrought heroic folly'; but Patrick Allen demonstrated how well this soliloquy works when the actor boldly addresses the audience, and Moshinsky throws away a valuable means of communication to no clear dramatic gain. The result is bewildering rather than menacing and tragic.

A more serious consequence of his tragic over-loading of the scenes occurs in Giacomo's attempted seduction of Innogen. When it comes to speaking verse, Robert Lindsay is no virtuoso like Eric Porter, but he does convey the point of Giacomo's convoluted speeches in this scene: his needling, incisive, edged delivery – often like rapier flicks – builds up, by calculated fits and starts, an atmosphere of obscure sexual suggestiveness. But whereas Peggy Ashcroft and Vanessa Redgrave recoiled from such suggestiveness in their Giacomos, emphasising Innogen's frank determination to cut through such devious verbiage, Helen Mirren becomes drawn in to the atmosphere that Giacomo is creating, and almost falls for his story about Posthumus at 'My lord, I fear,/ Has forgot Britain.' Giacomo's swift reply 'and himself' is followed by a little inarticulate cry from Innogen (I.vi.113-14). He sits beside her to press his advantage home, becoming more urgent and insistent during the next speech. It is a great advantage that this scene is virtually uncut; even Gaskill's very full text left out the obscure passage culminating in the phrase 'such boiled stuff/As well might poison poison' (I.vi.126-7), but Robert Lindsay whispers it rapidly and urgently, using it to lead into the crucial next phrase: 'Be revenged.' By now the camera has closed in on them as they sit face to face: she eagerly responds, catching his manner; for an instant she actually wants revenge. Giacomo shifts his tone and says 'revenge it' (I.vi.136) gently, as if to say 'It's easy!'; his dedicating himself to her sweet pleasure in the next line has never seemed so plausible, and she almost yields to him, almost allows him the kiss; 'What ho, Pisanio' is no exclamation but is gasped towards Giacomo's face, before she breaks away and denounces him; but she has not recovered: she is edgy and breathless in that speech. She has now become a fallen angel. Even so, Giacomo is thrown: he turns away, in the foreground of the shot, obviously shaken, and so he has to make a very quick recovery indeed to pretend that he was merely testing her, whereas for Eric Porter it was easy because of his lightweight playing of the whole scene. But that big transition is in the text; what is less surely in the text is an Innogen who almost yields to him.

In an article in the *Radio Times* at the time of the BBC showing (10 July 1983) Moshinsky provided more details about this interpretation than he gives in the BBC edition of the play:

> It's very clear that the character is susceptible and is almost seduced and that makes her feel enormously uneasy about herself. She's not a good person in a world of evil. The moment when she has to struggle she comes to understand something very uneasy about herself.... Giacomo's evil is not aggressive but cunningly wheedles the evil side out of other people. I always feel that when he says to Innogen, 'but the gods made you, unlike all others, chaffless', he is actually saying what she already knows – she should never have doubted Posthumus in the first place. And she doesn't feel chaffless (pure), she feels soiled. His evil depends on having made the other person guilty.

So, at the end of the scene, Giacomo directly challenges this sense of 'guilt'. Staring her straight in the eye, he refers to her faith in Posthumus as a 'judgement ... / Which *you know* cannot err' (I.vi.175-7). She cannot take his accusing gaze, and lowers her head in shamefaced evasion as he goes on to call her 'chaffless'. Helen Mirren handles the moment with great delicacy, and a certain *frisson* is created, but is it a legitimate interpretation of the text,

[69]

or is it an artificial screwing-up of the tension to make the scene fit Moshinsky's dark approach? He goes on: 'I thought of the play as being neurotic and exploratory and it seemed to me it needed an actress of great sexual voltage. Helen can act enormously complex sexual emotions at war with each other particularly well. She can take this character and make it undergo a crisis.' The give-away phrase here is '*make* it undergo a crisis'. The question is whether this crisis comes out of the text itself or is imposed upon it, and whether his talk of Innogen having an 'evil side', of being made 'guilty', is remotely appropriate.

However that may be, this interpretation leads straight into that of the bedroom scene which Moshinsky sees as 'a development of her mood. The character understands that she is possibly corruptible. Giacomo rising from the trunk while Innogen sleeps . . . thus becomes a figure of Innogen's dream, one of the "tempters of the night" from whom she prays to be guarded.' This scene is menacing from the very beginning in this version. There is thunder while Innogen lies on cushions beside the fire reading the tale of Tereus, though the shot is too brief to be fully registered by the viewer: it was clearer during the interval, which showed a 'still' of this moment (reproduced on page 59 of the BBC edition). Innogen is startled to her feet by the arrival of a particularly sinister lady-in-waiting, obviously an agent of the Queen, who hammers out perfectly neutral lines such as 'Please you, madam' to make them sound like threats. This is a simple example of how hard a director has to work to make the play seem neurotic; and the entire bedroom scene proceeds along these lines. As well as the sound of crickets, thunder rumbles throughout the scene, and Moshinsky again uses red lighting to suggest 'nightmare realism' and to illuminate Giacomo's dark figure contrasted with an Innogen bathed in golden light.

In other productions, this scene has seemed voyeuristic. In keeping with the bias of the production, Robert Lindsay goes further and finds it 'pornographic' (BBC edition, p. 24). He emerges naked from the trunk, which certainly establishes the 'potent sexual force' the director was aiming for, and increases the sense of potential rape. But if the scene is to be pornographic, why not go the whole hog and have Innogen naked too? After all, there is strong textual support for this: how else does Giacomo see the mole *under* her breast (II.iv.134), a matter on which Giacomo cannot afford to be inaccurate in the smallest detail, since it is his trump card in persuading Posthumus that he has won the wager? Robert Lindsay releases a lingering sigh before the reference to Tarquin, presumably to establish the supercharged sexuality of the interpretation. On television, of course, he can deliver the whole speech with a hushed intensity that scarcely rises above a whisper; but he also prefaces many phrases with a gasp: 'Cytherea – *oh* how bravely thou becom'st thy bed', '*Oh*, that I might touch', '*Oh*, on her left breast / A mole', and so on. By the end of the speech, this has become an irritating mannerism which detracts both from the speech itself (otherwise well delivered) and from the sense that he is acting out what she is dreaming about, which is presumably the point of all the gasping in the first place: 'You get a double take on the interior of her dream', as Moshinsky puts it; 'on television you get the opportunity of actually making the scene like her nightmare' (BBC edition, p.17). The surprising thing is that he doesn't actually succeed in suggesting that what we see is an externalisation of her dream; to do that, there would surely have had to be some focus on her face dissolving into Giacomo looming over her. The possibilities of television are in fact not exploited properly. The one real hint of what Moshinsky is trying to achieve comes at the end, with the reference to Tereus's rape of Philomel. On the phrase 'Philomel gave up', Innogen sighs deeply and stirs in her sleep, as if she were dreaming of giving in to Tereus/Giacomo. But that is all. It scarcely seems enough to establish the interpretation that Moshinsky is after.

'The removal of the bracelet is in fact a rape', says Moshinsky, and Innogen's distraction at the loss of it carries through into the next scene and motivates her behaviour towards Cloten. The Jacobean setting comes into its own in the presentation of the song 'Hark, hark, the lark'. Stephen Oliver sets this song as a fully-fledged aria, combining the two pieces of music that Cloten asks for into one: with its florid introduction for recorder, lute, violin and cello, and its verbal elaboration, it is at once 'a very excellent good-conceited thing', and 'a wonderful sweet air with admirable rich words to it' (II.iii.15-17), complete with trills to simulate the singing of the lark. Paul Jesson's Cloten, played in this scene at least as an upper-class bully, has a marvellous moment as he sits back with his glass of wine, wiping his sneering, dripping mouth, overtly contemptuous of his menials as they present this incomprehensible music that he has been 'advised' to give Innogen. During the song we are taken from his side of Innogen's bedroom door to her side as she searches in panic for the bracelet. When she emerges, therefore, she is in no mood to put up with Cloten, and very quickly comes to the boil when he smugly tells her 'You sin against / Obedience' (II.iv.108-9): she clenches her mouth as if to say 'Damn!' And when he goes on to insult Posthumus, she explodes with a seething '*Profane* fellow', and builds through this speech and the next to the calculated insult

> His meanest garment
> That ever hath but *clipped* his *body* is dearer
> In my respect than all the hairs above thee,
> Were they all made such men (II.iv.130-3)

which is spoken right into his face as a deliberate act of sexual provocation, especially on the words 'clipped' and 'body'. This motivates the harsh treatment that Cloten plans for her later, particularly the wish to rape her in her husband's clothes.

This sequence brings out another element of this Cloten. Paul Jesson says, 'we tried to make him unpredictable – dangerous in that sense. You never know what you're going to get from him – is he going to slap you across the face or burst into tears?' (BBC edition, p. 23). The production's emphasis on dark, overpowering sexuality recurs here: III.v is split into two scenes, so that Cloten's soliloquy 'I love and hate her' (III.v.70) begins a new sequence, which takes place in Innogen's bedroom; Cloten delivers it lying on her bed. There, Pisanio disturbs him, and Cloten veers rapidly between attacking Pisanio and scorning him: there is a nice exchange when Cloten is enumerating the commands he has given Pisanio. 'That is the second thing that I have commanded thee. The – '. He pauses; Pisanio volunteers 'Third?' 'Third', confirms Cloten, delivering the single syllable in a parody of an upper-class drawl, as if to say 'There was no need to tell me; I knew all the time' (III.v.149-50). Moshinsky emphasises Cloten's vanity by interpolating, at the end of the scene, an elaborate mime sequence. Surrounded by mirrors, and accompanied by a tinkling harpsichord, Cloten is dressed by Pisanio in Posthumus's clothes while he admires himself in the series of mirrors, as if he were Lord Foppington in Vanbrugh's *The Relapse*. There is a typically careless detail here. Pisanio has to wrench the doublet across Cloten's chest to get it to fasten, incurring an impatient slap from Cloten. It must have seemed an amusing local effect in rehearsal, but of course in suggesting that Cloten is too fat to fit into

Posthumus's doublet, it weakens the much insisted-upon physical similarity between their bodies once the head is off. The inconsistency is the more noticeable because, once dressed , Cloten then speaks the soliloquy from IV.i, 'How fit his garments serve me!', as far as 'What mortality is!' (IV.i.14-15). The rest of the soliloquy is spoken in its proper place.

This is the first of a large number of substantial cuts and rearrangements of the text in this production which radically alter the second half of the play. The BBC edition explains how this came about. The play

> seemed to require a peculiarly high level of emotional intensity in performance, and there did seem to be some passages, discovered in rehearsal of course, when it was considered impossible to sustain the necessary energy without severe cutting. . . . Once the action has moved to Wales there is a marked lowering of the energy level, so the second half of the play has been far more rigorously cut than the first – the prime victims of such surgery being the banished Belarius and his 'sons'. (p. 29)

This statement has awkward implications for the entire approach. It is the tragic interpretation, of course, that demands such a 'peculiarly high level of emotional intensity', and what that statement is in fact admitting is that the director has devised an approach which only works for some of the play. If the Belarius scenes demonstrated 'a marked lowering of the energy level' in rehearsal, that is likely to expose the weakness of the approach rather than of the scenes themselves since, as we have seen, they have been completely successful in other modern performances. Faced with the dilemma that a tragic interpretation provides him with no resource for performing an entire section of the play, the director simply cuts vast areas of it and rearranges the rest, instead of re-thinking his interpretation. Such circumstances deny the rural scenes, and especially the burial scene, the full impact that they normally have in performance. The cuts and rearrangements destroy their natural rhythm and substitute a new one of the director's devising. It is a tribute to the scenes that something of their quality survives such laceration.

The first Welsh scene is prefaced by a shot of an eagle in flight. This not only suggests the location but also anticipates – or so it seems – the descent of Jupiter. Belarius lives in a hermit's cell rather than a cave, to avoid exteriors in the studio as far as possible. Since there is no context for Arviragus's 'rain and wind beat dark

December' speech (III.iii.35-44), the last five lines are cut, one of the numerous extensive cuts that are made in addition to those marked in the BBC edition. Even in such unpropitious circumstances, and in spite of having to deliver it away from the camera rather than communicating directly with the viewer, Belarius's soliloquy takes hold, as it usually does. Michael Gough ruminates movingly on his past life, and his love for the princes is firmly expressed in the tenderness of 'myself . . . they take for natural father' (III.iii.106-7).

The burial scene is weakened both by the cuts and by a clash of styles. The landscape, with its plastic snow and its symbolic red lighting becoming bloodier with the beheading of Cloten, is at odds with such realistic sound effects as constantly chattering magpies. During the Cloten/Guiderius fight, there is a weird battle between two eagles in the sky above their heads: another anticipation of Jupiter? Arviragus's 'The bird is dead' cannot, I suppose, be as big a moment on televison as it is in the theatre, but here it goes for nothing: we simply cut from the snowy landscape to the interior of the cell, with Arviragus kneeling by Innogen's body. There follows a really staggering cut – nothing less than the whole of Arviragus's 'With fairest flowers' speech. After Guiderius has said 'If he be gone he'll make his grave a bed' (IV.ii. 217), the princes sing, not speak, 'Fear no more the heat o' th' sun.'

This is against the plainest instructions in the text, though of course these instructions are omitted here:

> Arviragus.   . . . let us, Polydore, though now our voices
> Have got the mannish crack, sing him to th' ground . . .
> Guiderius.   . . . I cannot sing. I'll weep, and word it with thee . . .
> Arviragus.   We'll speak it then. (IV.ii.236-43)

The argument that these lines represent a theatrical emergency, an actor's voice unexpectedly breaking, has always seemed to me wholly implausible. Shakespeare wants the 'song' spoken, so as to throw all attention on to the simple but highly charged words, an extension of the technique in 'The bird is dead' and Arviragus's flower speech. This introduction, far from being an apology for the lack of a song, prepares the audience for a spoken lament, a special kind of formal ritual celebrating the apparent victim and offering serene, simple consolation. In this way it builds upon, and develops, the sweetness and consolation in the flower speech, so Moshinsky's omission of that speech robs the scene of natural momentum and development, and the musical setting provides an effect quite different from the one implied by the scene, and

[74]

achieved in other productions.

Having said all that, I have to concede that the impact of this sung 'Fear no more' is nevertheless very great indeed. It almost compensates for the cutting of the flower speech because the sympathy expressed there is conveyed by the tender, plangent vocal setting, and also by the visual presentation. Innogen is in the foreground of the shot, with the back of her head to the camera. The princes kneel over her, fold her arms gently across her breast, and tenderly press flowers into her hands. Despite the directorial interference earlier, one of the most haunting and beautiful moments in Shakespeare is fully realised. Exactly why the image as the camera focuses on the flowers in Innogen's hands is so heartwrenching is a little hard to pin down. Perhaps it is that, when combined with the verbal beauty of the song, it seems to symbolise the princes' solicitous concern for Innogen. It may be felt that there can't be too much wrong with a production that gets so close to the emotional heart of the play as this. Unfortunately, however, the problems caused by the director's interference with the text soon surface again.

Moshinsky emphasises that Innogen's waking by the corpse is to be interpreted as a nightmare, 'which we shoot so we don't know where it happens: it's just she wakes up, and has this nightmare which is a kind of therapy for her' (p. 17). The technical drawbacks of the production are evident in Innogen's first waking lines: Helen Mirren makes mistakes in the first phrases and there obviously wasn't time for a re-take. Perhaps these slips don't matter too much, since Innogen is after all in a confused, half-drugged state. But that comes to seem a feeble excuse when this messy effect is compared with Gaskill's careful preparation for the awakening described in the previous chapter, or with Robin Phillips's analysis, quoted in the next chapter, of how Shakespeare has written the opening lines very carefully to help the actress: it is clear that Mirren's and Moshinsky's sheer carelessness over verbal detail cannot do justice to Shakespeare's achievement here. The impression is of the actress feeling for the lines rather than of Innogen gradually awakening. Mirren's incomplete control over the scene is further exposed in the high-pitched, uneasy delivery of the plea for 'as small a drop of pity / As a wren's eye' and of 'Where is thy head? Where's that?' Ay me, where's that? (IV.ii.306-7, 323).

It would be unfair to suggest that Helen Mirren rises to none of the soliloquy. She uses her realistic style of playing to bring off a daring interpretation of possibly the trickiest passage, Innogen's positive identification of Cloten's body as Posthumus's. As she moves from horror-struck nightmare to the realisation that she really is beside a headless corpse, that her experience is 'not imagined, felt', the 'truth' dawns slowly: 'The garments of Posthumus?' And then she gradually begins to nod with increasing certainty as she proceeds with the identification: 'I know the shape of's leg; this is his hand', and so on. This expression of certainty makes the point that what we know to be factually untrue is nevertheless entirely real, and horrific, for her. And she clinches this 'nightmare realism' by dipping her hands in the bloody neck and thoroughly daubing her face, as the Oxford editors think she should. The effect is powerful, but in a repellent rather than a moving way. The savagery of the spectacle certainly makes Moshinsky's point that this is a 'kind of therapy' for Innogen; after this experience, future happiness will be hard-won and the more valued.

But Moshinsky almost ruins this point by not allowing her to proceed at once with the rest of the scene. There is a cut to Caius Lucius talking to the Soothsayer in a completely different location (IV.ii.346-355), then to Cymbeline lamenting the illness of the Queen, who groans in bed in the background (IV.iii), then to the first half (but only the first half) of Posthumus's returning soliloquy (V.i.1-17) before poor Innogen is allowed her (severely abbreviated) meeting with Caius Lucius. This chopping about seems entirely pointless; moreover, the director seems to lack the courage of his convictions in the haphazard execution of the rearrangement. The changed order as actually shown does not wholly correspond with the rearrangement given in the BBC edition, and there are inconsistencies even within his own plan: Innogen plays her soliloquy inside the cell, where the princes left her, identified by a candle; but Caius Lucius finds her by the body outside in the snow. How did she and Cloten get there? What is gained by such inconsistency?

Since the production itself provides no answers to these questions, we have to turn to the BBC edition for an explanation from the director:

> it's not very good if you have long development takes: sometimes you want to go to Pisanio, back to Cloten, back to Posthumus, then on to Innogen. The best thing to do is not to have long speeches but to intercut them, so you get four or five speeches, cut in the middle

> and relocated in different places so that they can be done as it were simultaneously. (p. 20)

The obvious problem with this is that Shakespeare has written the scenes in, as it were, 'long development takes', sequentially not simultaneously. What is missing from Moshinsky's version of the play at least serves to point up the sure, skilful development, in pace and rhythm, of Shakespeare's own version of the burial scene, from the lyrical pathos of the princes' formal burial rites to the violence of Innogen's emotional crisis beside the body and thence to her resolve to overcome her despair, which starts the play's upward curve to reunion and reconciliation.

That process is, in the text, reinforced by the soliloquy which Posthumus delivers on his return. Michael Pennington, who plays Posthumus, obviously grasps the point of it when he says:

> What is genuinely original about the whole role is that he forgives [Innogen] while still believing her to be technically guilty, which neither Leontes nor Othello do. He actually is able to say, 'Whatever she may have done I am the one to blame for having tried to kill her.' It seems to me to be enlightened and original and modern and absolutely true to life. (BBC edition, p. 25)

Quite so; but Pennington is prevented from communicating this fully in his performance by more interference from the director:

> I've done something I haven't done before, which is to take a speech and cut it in the middle and relocate part of it. The first half of Posthumus' soliloquy . . . is contemplative [talking of Innogen]. The second half is active [he takes off his Italian clothes and disguises himself as a British peasant]. What I've decided to do is – the first half is set in a tent, and we're close to him, but for the second half, when he disrobes himself, he goes outside. In television I can cut within a speech to a different location and not worry about continuity: it's like a time jump. (p. 20)

But a director should 'worry about continuity'. Posthumus needs to be re-established in the play as strongly as possible, and the uninterrupted soliloquy achieves this. To chop it up makes it impossibly difficult to focus attention on Posthumus again, the more so since he now looks so different, with his shaven head and peasant rags. Since the battle and the Posthumus/Giacomo duel are omitted altogether, the viewer only learns about such important events from Posthumus's subsequent narrative (or part of it).

Quite apart from the narrative confusion, the director's methods have a disturbing effect on Michael Pennington's performance as Posthumus. Perhaps instinctively realising that he has to re-establish the role with no help from the director, he resorts to the verbal mannerisms that he has used in other productions when uncertain about his effects, especially a habit of dwelling eccentrically upon phrases and drawing them out excessively which slows down the scenes unbearably. It is clearest when he reads Jupiter's prophecy: eyes twitching, he reads hesitantly, gropingly, as if he were dim-witted, and this, combined with his destitute appearance (complete with the 'naked breast' that Cymbeline mentions at V.vi.4) suggests a bizarre mixture of the mad Lear, poor Tom, and the derelicts of Samuel Beckett. In these scenes, he seems to be a completely different character from the deluded tragic hero he presents in the first half, not a repentant version of that earlier figure.

Posthumus is on screen almost continuously from the middle of his returning soliloquy to the end of the Jupiter scene, so the production seems to be building to a big climax in that scene, especially in view of what look like pointers towards it – eagles in flight, ominously rumbling thunder throughout the entire sequence from Innogen's awakening to the appearance of Jupiter. In addition, Moshinsky interprets the scene, like the trunk and corpse scenes, on two levels. On the objective level, 'the intervention of the gods' prevents the play ending tragically, while on the subjective level the action is the externalisation of Posthumus's dream. But this dual view is not communicated in performance. The director talks much about using 'filmic techniques' to suggest 'the interior' of characters' dreams, but neither in the bedroom scene nor here does he actually use them. There is no suggestion that what we are seeing is Posthumus's dream of Jupiter on an eagle. Instead, there is another bald jump from Posthumus falling asleep manacled in his chair to a close-up of Marius Goring as his father glaring balefully and accusingly up at Jupiter: a more corporeal spirit would be hard to imagine. There is no hint that these are dream figures: Posthumus's family merely gather round his chair while Michael Hordern's urbane Jupiter stands looking down on them in the foreground of the shot. And astonishingly, after those earlier eagles, there isn't one here where the text asks for it. We should not perhaps expect theatrical virtuosity on television; we are surely entitled to expect equivalent technical virtuosity in television terms. With two Shakespearian veterans of the authority of Marius Goring and Michael Hordern the scene can hardly fail to have some impact, but it is not the climax that the play, and even this production, lead us to expect.

Moshinsky carries his principle of fragmentation into the final scene. This is cut very little, but continuity is avoided by presenting it 'not as a group scene, but a series of individual small scenes' (p. 26), almost entirely using close-up. To keep the tragic treatment going, or at least to avoid genuine repentance or reconciliation, Robert Lindsay plays Giacomo's repentance as what he calls 'a lie – I think he's getting off the hook extremely successfully' (p. 24). In a characteristically perverse decision, bearing in mind how many beautiful lines he has omitted earlier, Moshinsky includes the whole of Giacomo's convoluted account of his wager – and he has staged it with the utmost clumsiness. Cymbeline and Giacomo face one another across the inevitable table. Trying to get him to talk sense, Cymbeline grabs Giacomo and pulls him across the table, and in that awkward position Lindsay throws away the speech in a combination of inaudibility and gabbling. Catching the disease, Michael Pennington grovels on the floor and rants, dragging out his self-laceration so that it seems to go on for ever. It is no wonder, under such circumstances, that the two best moments are not verbal ones: a brief shot of Innogen simply closing her eyes as she understands Giacomo's plot, and the princes clinging to Belarius rather than be parted from him. Michael Gough's superbly rounded characterisation of Belarius is very moving: he and the princes alone bring some humanity into the scene – a good example of the material resisting the director's interference.

The BBC edition claims that the textual 'abridgement and rearrangement has been the result of wanting to make a complex tale clearer by ridding it of comparative irrelevancies and highlighting certain moments and themes' (p. 29). The one certainty about this treatment is that it does not make the play clearer. The director in fact has done it the disservice of making it seem far more confused than it really is by disrupting its own narrative sequence. The arbitrary rearrangement makes it much harder to follow the story than anything the full text would have provided. Besides, the apparent 'irrelevancies' mentioned are only irrelevant to Moshinsky's tragic interpretation. They are part of the life of the play, and it should be the director's job to interpret them, rather than to give up and simply leave them out. One of their functions is to 'highlight certain moments', as this production claimed to do by cutting; but Gaskill's version demonstrated that the highlighting of certain moments happens anyway, rising naturally out of the full text, because Shakespeare's own manipulation of structure and rhythm, his 'irrelevancies' even, work specifically to that end.

Since this television version of *Cymbeline* is easily available, it will inevitably be more influential than any other modern production. It has therefore been necessary to dwell upon the ways in which it falls short of most theatre productions, and certainly of those discussed in detail here. It gives only an approximate idea of the play in performance, and its contribution to our understanding is largely achieved in negative ways. Its chief significance for interpretation is that it sharply exposes the limitation of a tragic approach. This provides some striking local effects in the two wager scenes and in the Giacomo/Innogen scene. But already in the last of these the text has to be seriously distorted to suggest not only that Innogen is ambiguous and fallible, but that she has the potential for 'evil'. The tragic line gives the actor of Posthumus no way of coping with the modulations of tone in the jealous soliloquy, or with the repentance scenes, where he has to be played as a completely different character. The text is not *that* inconsistent, as other Posthumuses have shown. Above all, the tragic interpretation provides no resource for staging the pastoral scenes, roughly half of the play, as Moshinsky admits by his savage cutting and alterations.

But the real problem with the production is that Moshinsky has failed to communicate his own interpretation adequately. Whether through lack of nerve, of studio time, or of the necessary skill, his trunk, burial, and Jupiter scenes do not in fact give the impression of events happening simultaneously before us and in the minds of the heroine and hero. The idea is simply not made to work in television terms. So it is interesting that in Robin Phillips's production at Stratford, Ontario in 1986, these three central scenes gave *exactly* the impression of being an externalisation of the sleepers' dreams, a natural extension of their experiences during the play. This in part reflects the difference between a hit-and-miss director and one who combines great flair with a fastidious care for detail. But it suggests another contrast too. It is significant that Phillips's production was carried out with the utmost theatrical virtuosity on a large open stage. Perhaps this play is too essentially of the theatre to work on television.

CHAPTER V

Cymbeline on the open stage: Productions by Jean Gascon (1970) and Robin Phillips (1986), Stratford, Ontario

It is a great relief to turn from the claustrophobic atmosphere of the television version to the open spaces of the Festival Theatre at Stratford, Ontario. Since its foundation in 1953, this festival has made several notable contributions to the theatrical interpretation of Shakespeare. During this time it has only performed *Cymbeline* twice, in 1970 and 1986, but both performances were outstandingly successful, enthusiastically received by both press and public. Any account of productions at this theatre must begin with a brief description of the stage. A huge platform, with steps at the front, juts out into the audience, who surround it on three sides in a very wide arc. At the back of this platform, steps lead to an upper level, supported by pillars. There is an acting space and central entry beneath this balcony. When empty, this vast open stage can suggest great isolation; as it fills up, it offers great opportunities for activity and ceremony. Full or empty, it demands a boldly extrovert acting style, and great imagination and skill from its directors and designers. It tends to stamp its personality on performers, who must either exploit its advantages or find a way to counteract its vastness. Jean Gascon's production in 1970 broadly followed the first course, Robin Phillips's in 1986 the second.

Tanya Moiseiwitsch, who designed Jean Gascon's production, had also designed the stage itself in 1953, and having devised an acting area which she considered appropriate for Shakespeare, she not surprisingly left it as it was for *Cymbeline*, with no further set apart from a tapestry suspended from the balcony for Rome, some swagging under the balcony to suggest Belarius's cave, huge banners for the British and Roman factions, and, most important, a small platform built out over the steps at the front of the stage. This was used to provide a focus for the bedroom, burial, and Jupiter scenes, with either Innogen or Posthumus lying upon it, and this served to link the three scenes together. The costumes were in weaves, wool, and fur for the Britons, with arm-bands and beads; the Romans wore their customary classical armour; Giacomo's white shirt and flowing cape were deliberately showier than the rest. The Queen was a black-clad witch, with a raven perched on her shoulder to intensify the sinister associations; Cloten was a grotesque, but not excessively so. In general, the visual effect suggested *Cymbeline* as a reader might imagine it, a remote, romantic Ancient Britain, but not so specific that the Renaissance elements could not be accommodated within it. Indeed, both design and production worked so easily that, as with Gaskill's version which this one resembled in its bold simplicity, the supposed perversities of the play seemed much exaggerated.

Most of the production was clear and vigorous. The performances were strong and extrovert rather than subtle, making the points of each scene swiftly and unfussily. The two Giacomo/Posthumus scenes worked particularly well, getting the play off to an excellent start. They were as tense and exciting as in the television version, though of course much less intimate, using the larger gestures and more rhetorical vocal style that the open stage encourages. Leo Ciceri (Giacomo) was a master of this. He began the wager scene sitting on the steps at the front of the stage, breaking in on the conversation between the Frenchman and Posthumus and so drawing Posthumus's attention to him with an ostentatious, provoking 'Can we with manners ask what was the difference?' (I.iv.51-2). At once the tension was established between the two of them and when Giacomo swore to carry out the wager, Posthumus's 'Will you?' was quietly testing, rather than outraged. The handling of Giacomo's attempted seduction of Innogen demonstrated how the open stage can be used to point a scene, provided that an actor knows how to handle it. Ciceri circled round the outside of the stage as he delivered 'What, are men mad?' and the other speeches intended to bewilder Innogen (I.vi.33ff.) out into the house, intended for her ears but directed away from her, before he gradually closed in on her – though an unusually tough and resilient Innogen kept him at arm's length.

The shape and conditions of this stage are based on roughly Elizabethan principles, and so they tend to invite speculation about Elizabethan staging. The bedroom scene was a case in point. Older critics, such as Granville-Barker, supposed that the whole scene took place far upstage, on an 'inner stage' under the balcony; this would mean that the scene would have been separated from the audience by the empty main stage. One only has to think for a moment about the barrier thus created to realise how preposterously impractical the whole 'inner stage' theory was, and it is now thoroughly discredited. The Folio's stage direction 'Enter Innogen in her bed', presumably implies that the bed was either carried on or, more likely, 'thrust out' from a central 'discovery space' upstage, a practice mentioned in other stage directions of the period. The Textual Companion to the Oxford Shakespeare makes the interesting additional suggestion that the trunk 'might have been pushed up through the trap, which would permit easier entrance and exit for Giacomo, and supply a potent visual image of his ascent from and descent into "hell"'. Then, at the end of the scene, the trunk could sink back through the trap as the bed was thrust back into the 'discovery space' (Stanley Wells and Gary Taylor, eds., *William Shakespeare: A Textual Companion*, 1987, p. 605).

Clifford Leech, however, in an article prompted by the 1970 Ontario production, still wondered if Innogen did not remain upstage 'in some kind of "discovery space" and if Giacomo, on emerging from the trunk, did not at first advance onto the main stage as he talked of her and her chamber's embellishments. It might be effective if Innogen were kept remote here and Giacomo moved back and forth as he commented on what he saw' (*The Triple Bond*, ed. J. G. Price, 1975, p. 77). It is hard to imagine anything *less* effective, since such aimless wandering about would rob the scene of its focus on Innogen, indeed of any focus at all, and it seems astonishing that Leech apparently failed to learn from the staging of the scene in this Ontario production. The bed was placed on the built-out platform at the very front of the stage, with Innogen's head facing the central section of the audience, so that Giacomo approached and addressed her and the audience at the same time, providing an intenser concentration even than in

Gaskill's version. The sharp focus gained by such staging makes it inconceivable that so intimately written a scene should be positioned anywhere other than in the closest proximity to the audience.

Leech objected to the playing of Cloten 'as a figure of grotesque fun throughout', adding 'I do not know how Cloten should be acted; I doubt whether the figure in its full many-sidedness can be satisfactorily acted' (pp. 81-2). Readers can refer to my description of Clive Revill's and Clive Swift's performances and draw their own conclusions as to whether the part can be satisfactorily acted or not; but it is certainly true that Robin Gammell's Cloten in this production was a simpler character than either of those, more primitive, more a figure out of romance. The musicians deliberately guyed 'Hark, hark, the lark', and Leech is quite right to object that 'it is a foolish trick of the stage to justify [Cloten] by making the musicians inadequate' (p.80), a mistake made in other productions too, including Gaskill's, his sole lapse from grace. But Leech's dismissal of this Cloten as simply a figure of grotesque fun is unjust to his playing of III.v, where he was also a figure of dangerous violence; and he made every point about wearing Posthumus's clothes in revenge for Innogen's earlier insult. This was close to Moshinsky's treatment of the episode, but unlike Moshinsky, Gascon took the greatest pains to make the story-telling very clear indeed throughout, but especially from this point on, where it is becoming especially tortuous.

He was greatly helped in this by the fact that the two princes were perhaps the best actors in the production, and outstanding speakers of verse. So, once the strong performances of Giacomo, Posthumus, and Cloten had launched the main plot, these princes were able to build upon what had been established: the gradually increasing impact of the production, as in Gaskill's version, attested once again to the quality and importance of these roles. Stephen Markle and Leon Pownall were almost entirely naked, very much 'hot summer's tanlings' (IV.iv.29), and they played the princes as noble savages, a point brilliantly made after the Cloten/ Guiderius fight which drew (underisive) laughter and applause, and which was followed by Guiderius's displaying of the head with bloodthirsty cries of sheer ecstasy. This was one side of the 'noble savage'; the other was an impulsive tenderness towards Fidele, even to the point of caressing and fondling him/her. This made the best possible build-up to the dirge, which was the finest in my experience. They placed Innogen on the promontory–platform, in a precise echo of the bedroom positioning. They began the dirge kneeling, as is customary; but then they rose, with arms out-stretched to her and to the audience, warding off the evil spirits and the 'exorcisers'. The dirge was magnificently spoken, and the audience mesmerised. The play's technique, summarised by Leech, was clearer than ever: Shakespeare can take the tortuous plot 'beyond the credible while at the same time exploring a genuine human anguish' (p. 86).

These princes, and the image they presented, made a vital con-tribution to the climactic battle and final scenes. As the Roman army crossed the stage, Posthumus turned back from it for his soliloquy. He tore off his Roman cloak to 'suit' himself 'as does a Briton peasant' (V.i.23.-4) – that is, he appeared almost as naked as the princes, like them an image of 'less without and more within' (V.i.33). There was a tremendous impression of four naked figures defeating the armoured might of Rome, and the audience responded with more applause, as they did to the Jupiter scene. For his dream, Posthumus lay chained to the promontory at the front of the stage; the ghosts simply walked on in half-light; then came the production's great *coup de théâtre*. There had been rumbl-ing thunder throughout; a sudden flash of lightning revealed a Greek-style Jupiter astride a gigantic eagle on the upper level. Both this scene and the battle exploited the 'Elizabethan' features of this stage to good effect. For sheer imagination and visual splen-dour, neither scene had quite the impact of the stagings in Gaskill's production, though each came near to it in a similar style.

The finale began with a theatrical novelty: Cornelius announced that 'the Queen comes crawling hither, beseeching you to hear her testimony'. She appeared with wild Ophelia hair, spoke the lines that Cornelius attributes to her, died on stage, and was bundled unceremoniously away to audience laughter and applause: so much for wicked witches. There was further thunder during the scene, including a terrific clap when Innogen asked Giacomo about the ring. The influence of Jupiter was clearly felt; his prophecy was beginning to come true. Gascon's assistant director Michael Bawtree, in his programme notes, also made the relevant point that the upward movement of the play begins *before* the appear-ance of Jupiter:

the change from chaos to miraculous resolution ... begins in the battle, when ... the boys join the fight. Some said they were angels, and Posthumus tells us how men that were slain (or appeared slain) rose up and routed the Romans. We felt this should be a truly miraculous moment ... which leads then to the Jupiter vision .... The dead men will actually rise, and the boys *will* be angels of a kind.

A similar point, drawing on the same textual evidence, has independently been made by Marion Lomax in her *Stage Images and Traditions*, 1987:

Posthumus's last stand is in a lane 'Close by the battle, ditched, and walled with turf' (V.v.14), [and] this is reminiscent of a grave. Later ... it is said of Belarius and the two brothers whom he met there, ''Tis thought the old man and his sons were angels' (V.v.85). According to the imagery, Posthumus's search for death leads him right into the grave (as it does Innogen) and then delivers him from it. (p. 117)

Here is further persuasive evidence to link Posthumus's traumatic experiences with Innogen's, a point developed in the second Ontario production. Both Lomax and Bawtree make the point that the princes, whether as 'angels' or simply as virtuous heroes, contribute to Posthumus's progress towards reunion with Innogen as they do to Innogen's with him. At the end, the princes joined hands with their sister and with their brother-in-law and comrade-in-arms. This gradually led into the magnificent ending, with the whole cast slowly catching the sense of reconciliation and gradually joining hands, as their ensigns were interlocked, and a great banner with a sun emblem displayed overhead. Perhaps no *Cymbeline* has caught quite so securely the sense of reunion and renewal that is often thought central to Shakespeare's late plays. The emotion on stage swept over the audience too, who regularly responded with cheering ovations. That these were for the play as much as the production is suggested by the fact that there was a similar response to the second Ontario production, a very different kind of production indeed.

In 1986, Robin Phillips reacted sharply against the primitive–mythical style of a production like Jean Gascon's. Shakespeare, he said, 'is not writing about people running around Stonehenge', and his initial intention was to set it in the Jacobean period 'because of the connections with and through James I and the history of the times'. In particular, he wanted to focus upon the war:

> I felt I had to find a period when war meant something in the sense
> that it could have happened to someone I knew . . . To Shakespeare's
> audience, there would have been that pull. Although he set it in
> ancient Britain, it would have been dressed in what was, to them,
> modern dress. They would have been watching an ancient British
> story that reminded them of the immmediately preceding wars that
> had happened between England and Spain so they would have said,
> 'my family has been through this problem'. That is the quality we
> must recreate with today's audience.

In order to do that, he chose to set the play not in the present but
in the late 1930s and early 1940s. (All quotations from Robin Phillips in this chapter are from the theatre's publicity or from Robert
Gaines's book about the 1986 season, *John Neville Takes Command*,
1987, pp.257-85.)

The theatre's publicity caught the tone of the production: 'as
the skies over Europe darken with approaching war, a commoner
wins the heart of the heir to the British throne'. The Innogen/Post-
humus relationship was presented as a kind of reversal of the affair
between Edward VIII and Mrs Simpson which led to the king's
abdication. Phillips aimed to place the events of the play in a context which the audience could recognise. The period was re-created
with Phillips's customary fastidious attention to every last detail
of staging. It certainly cast an interesting new light on much of
the play, but I couldn't help feeling that the visual allusions were
more accessible to an English audience than to a Canadian one.
The tone was very English indeed.

This context gave assistance to the two characters most in need
of it, Cymbeline and the Queen. They were as far from the
archetypal fairy-tale figures of Hall's or Gascon's versions as from
the Medicis of Moshinsky's. Grasping Emrys Jones's point that
these characters must be figure-heads, and that Cymbeline in particular must simply be 'the great Western King', Phillips found
instantly recognisable thirties equivalents for them which would
help a modern audience to accept them as symbolic figures. Cymbeline was clearly George V, wearing a variety of naval uniforms
and shooting outfits, attended by grooms and gamekeepers on his
country estates. By this means Phillips presented him as an image
of royalty which discouraged the raising of too many awkward
psychological questions. For the Queen, however, a double image
was created, appropriate to so duplicitous a character. In public,
she was Queen Mary, solicitously supporting Cymbeline/George V
against foreign invaders; but in private, she became a bluestocking

lady doctor in a white lab coat, who had obviously converted an area of the palace kitchens into a makeshift laboratory where she could assess the 'several virtues and effects' of her poisons (I.v.23). If her public image was based on history, her private one was theatrical: this Queen recalled the eccentric sanatorium owner in Friedrich Dürrenmatt's *The Physicists*, not just in her white-coated appearance but also in her brisk manner. When, for instance, she mentioned the flowers which would provide some of the ingredients for her 'compounds', 'the violets, cowslips, and the primroses' (I.v.83), this was no lyrical line. Susan Wright's mouth curled in contempt and distaste as she spoke it, as if to say 'cowslips! for heaven's sake!' There was an interesting contrast between this performance and Joan Miller's in Peter Hall's 1957 production. Whereas Joan Miller made a big humorous point of switching in one breath from her hatred of Innogen to innocent lyricism, Susan Wright made the phrase consistent with the private 'face' of her Queen, a ruthless woman to whom the beauties of nature existed solely to serve her purposes, and this attitude to the natural world had parallels elsewhere in the production. With such a strong performer in the role, Phillips followed Gascon in providing the audience with an emphatic reminder of her malign presence in the final scene, not this time physically but vocally: as Cornelius reported her dying speech, his voice gave way to her strikingly individual tones coming over the amplification system.

A very specifically English atmosphere was created for Cymbeline's court: a stultifying, musty country-house society between the wars, a society already dying on its feet and about to be swept away almost entirely by the Second World War. Elegant metal gates attached to the pillars supporting the balcony enclosed the back area of the stage: they suggested the wicket to a small village church belonging to a great house; beyond it were graves, partly overgrown. Phillips achieved two things with these gates. First, they helped to counteract the vastness of the stage for more intimate exchanges; when vastness was needed, they were simply opened out again. The inspiration for the design was Turner's painting of Tintern Abbey in ruins, because Phillips wanted the sense of a world in which the man-made was becoming overgrown by nature, the natural world reasserting itself. This approach would seem to promise well for the Welsh scenes, but these were curiously presented after the fastidious realism of the court. Belarius's cave was oddly suggested by the use of tall metal cages enclosing animal skulls, presumably the trophies of the hunt. It seemed perverse to imply that Belarius and the princes were taming the natural world, whereas that world was beginning to take over the corrupt court. The decadent English aristocracy was contrasted with another kind of decadence in Italy, where the civilians lounged indolently in clubs or on the lido, and where the military were Mussolini's Fascist storm-troopers in trench-coats.

The new period worked on two levels. Phillips emphasised that the play shows 'recognisable human behaviour and how from reasonable beginnings we can go from love and care of each other to aggression and violence ... and finally to open warfare and murder and then back again to be reminded of generosity and sensitivity'. So the public nightmare of a world rushing headlong into a cataclysmic war was reflected on the private level by internal violence and especially by the personal nightmares of Innogen and Posthumus, with Giacomo as the catalyst in each case. In the scenes between these three, the range of the production underlined that of the play itself. The realism of the approach lent great psychological complexity and conviction to these scenes, while the conscious theatricality, sometimes amounting to sensationalism, of Phillips's staging of the three dreams or nightmares – the trunk, corpse, and Jupiter scenes – made Shakespeare's own technique clearer than ever: both play and production used shock effect to jolt the audience into an extra awareness of the characters' emotions, presented in extreme terms.

The realism was particularly effective in the two scenes between Giacomo and Posthumus. The wager took place in an Italian gentlemen's club. Giacomo was a part of this lounging, indolent world, but also something more sinister, psychotic beneath his contained exterior. He veered between a man-of-the-world cynicism encouraged by the society around him and a needling insinuation with which he taunted Posthumus. The two of them inevitably clashed, for Posthumus was a stiff-backed English prig who was thoroughly ill-at-ease both with this casual society and with himself, a point tellingly made when he exploded very early in the scene at the suggestion that Innogen might be imperfect: 'You are mistaken!' (I.iv.80). This was a very different handling of the line from Michael Pennington's confident, explanatory response to Giacomo in the television version.

Posthumus's inner uncertainty was clearer still in their second scene together. Even before Giacomo entered, Posthumus's jumpy unease as he declared that he felt 'bold her honour / Will remain hers' (II.iv.2-3) belied his confident words. The contrast between tense, buttoned-up Briton and lounging Italian was made visually: Posthumus wore a stuffy suit and pullover even on the lido, while Giacomo lay on the floor in a yellow bathrobe, entirely relaxed and apparently uninterested in discussing the wager, thus compelling the anxious Posthumus to raise the matter himself. He exploded as early in this scene as in his previous one, on 'Make not, sir, / Your loss your sport' (II.iv.47-8). After it, he bit his lip anxiously, as he realised that he had gone too far too soon and revealed his insecurity – an insecurity that Giacomo exploited with consummate ease. He stretched out on his back to describe 'the roof o' th' chamber (II.iv. 87), thus suggesting to Posthumus that it was from that position on Innogen's bed that he was able to see it so well. This was particularly upsetting for Posthumus who had spent so little time in that room. He might have been rash and priggish, but he was also vulnerable, and this was the key to his handling of the following soliloquy. This became the utterance of a man whose self-confidence, precarious at best, was utterly shattered; the tricky cynicism emerged as a desperate attempt by someone on the brink of tears to avoid complete collapse by indulging in clichés about women's inconstancy. The interpretation was cleverly thought out and persuasively performed by Joseph Ziegler. Canadian audiences are even less willing than English ones to listen line by line; nevertheless they took all the points here and responded to the soliloquy with applause.

Although Martha Burns's Innogen was also vulnerable to Giacomo's sexual insinuations, she coped with them much better than her husband. She was mettlesome and quick-witted, on her guard throughout: 'My lord, I fear, / Has forgot Britain' (I.vi.113-14) was neither gullible nor heartbroken but a sharp, suspicious question. Colm Feore handled Giacomo's tortuous speeches in this scene with a suave ease that caught all their suggestive, loaded sexuality, and this led logically into the bedroom scene, which was the first theatrical *tour de force* of the production. Innogen's lady-in-waiting put her book on top of the trunk, so that Giacomo had to open one half of the lid, find the book, and secure it from falling, before he could open both halves of the lid and emerge into the room. The manoeuvre in itself created tension, which was greatly increased when Giacomo whispered the entire speech, using a throat microphone. This ostentatiously theatrical device might have distracted attention from the text to the device, but Colm Feore performed it with such bravura that it had the opposite effect. It established an extraordinary hushed tension in the theatre, and so ensured maximum concentration upon what Giacomo was saying and doing. And in the process it underlined the similar purpose of Shakespeare's own virtuoso theatricality. Also, because Feore emerged from the trunk close to the audience, we in a sense moved with him to the bed and to Innogen, so that the voyeuristic aspect of the scene was intensified.

As the scene progressed, Innogen seemed in greater danger than she has seemed in any other modern production, especially when Giacomo drew the bedclothes completely off her and straddled her before kissing the mole on her breast, as he subsequently tells Posthumus that he did (II.iv.137). Not surprisingly, she almost woke; but her troubled, uneasy sleep was not, or not wholly, the result of Giacomo's attentions. As she twisted and turned, she appeared very disturbed: perhaps she was dreaming of Tereus's rape of Philomel which she had been reading about. This graphic staging implied much more strongly than Moshinsky's that the near-rape was an externalising of her nightmare. It also carried another suggestion. Giacomo wore jodhpurs, which gave the additional impression of 'riding' her in the sexual sense; and as her body twisted and buckled beneath his, the distinction between near-rape and actual rape began to seem very thin. As Clifford Leech put it in discussing the previous Ontario version, 'innocent as she is, the two of them do, after a fashion, share the night' together (p. 77). This impression was stronger here than in any of the other productions I have seen. Was it, therefore, as Robert Lindsay thinks the scene is, pornographic? Not exactly; but Innogen seemed much more soiled than usual, far more than in the television version, for all Lindsay's nakedness. But pornographic or not, the scene held the audience throughout, and at the end, when the almost unbearable tension was released, they applauded Colm Feore, who had caught both the sophisticated theatricality and the emotional realities which it focuses upon: desire, obsessive sexuality, a rape that is not quite a rape. What he missed, and this applies to Phillips's interpretation as a whole, was the lyrical beauty of the speech, and therefore Giacomo's tribute to Innogen herself.

The lack of response to the beauty of the language, and the cutting of some of it, was much more damaging in the Welsh scenes.

They did not strike a balance with the 'main' plot as they had done in the previous Ontario production. The impetus of Phillips's version sagged during these scenes, partly because he presented them in a totally different style from the rest of the production. In jarring contrast to the clear, rational, daylight world of the 1930s which he had so carefully established, the princes were near-naked savages with long hair and bows and arrows. My first reaction was that Phillips had given up on the scenes and decided to present them as in more conventional stagings. The naked princes of Gascon's version fitted the primitive world created in that production; but here, one wondered why Belarius couldn't have found them some clothes in a Welsh village store in the 1930s. Such a prosaic reaction pinpoints a difficulty in updating this play. Whereas the political situation lent itself easily to a realistic twentieth-century setting, it proved much harder to find a modern equivalent for Belarius's preference for a contemplative life in rural surroundings which have enabled him to pay 'more pious debts to heaven' (III.iii.72) than was possible in the political world.

But it gradually became clear, when Innogen barged into their world wheeling a bicycle and wearing the uniform and tin hat of a British 'Tommy', that they were intended to be images of natural man uncorrupted by the clothes and institutions of twentieth-century civilisation. The clash of styles was obviously deliberate, and created a moment of delightful incongruity: the princes and Innogen were amazed at each other's appearance, and the friendly 'brotherly' punches they exchanged drew much sympathetic laughter from the audience. It seemed natural for these princes to use phrases like 'the night to th' owl and morn to th' lark less welcome' (III.vi.91), and equally natural for them to use phrases like 'we are beastly . . . like warlike as the wolf' (III. iii.40-1), which expressed the darker side of the natural man's spontaneity, the violence and brutality, even bestiality, which culminates in the killing of Cloten.

Even so, neither this episode, nor the burial and Innogen's waking, had the impact of the previous Ontario version, partly because Phillips's direction became curiously mannered in this scene. Wailing, unearthly voices filled the air, and the princes chanted the dirge like some strange primitive rite. As they did so, autumn leaves gradually floated down from the flies to the stage. Phillips believed 'that the falling leaves forced the audience to listen more closely to the lines' (Gaines, p. 279). In other words, the falling leaves were a selfconscious theatrical effect designed, like Giacomo's throat microphone, to concentrate attention on the text. But unlike the microphone, the leaves and other effects in the burial scene did not work like that. The audience shifted uneasily, and there was a definite impression of a production losing its way. Part of the trouble was that the surreal staging had so little to do with the detailed realism to which the audience had grown accustomed in the earlier part of the production. These effects might have fitted a staging that emphasised the 'Stonehenge' element for which Phillips expressed such scorn, but they seemed incongruous here. Another problem was that the use of the leaves was forced and affected, as if Phillips did not trust the simplicity of Shakespeare's evocation of the natural world that is so vital in this scene. He cut Arviragus's lines about the charitable robin covering the body with furred moss (IV.ii.225-30), and by having the dirge chanted, he robbed it of its heart-catching simplicity. The air of elaborate contrivance was at odds with the directness of the language, and the actors playing the princes lacked the technique to bring off the interpretation.

This was not a good preparation for Innogen's waking soliloquy. Although the surreal atmosphere prevailed, Phillips had obviously thought carefully about how to play the opening section of the soliloquy in realistic terms. When Innogen wakes up and sees the body, Phillips points out,

> The first line [Shakespeare] gives Innogen is not about the dead body, but about the flowers strewn around it. It is as if he is saying to the actor, 'Don't scream. The audience will laugh at you. First of all notice the flowers while the character gains control of her emotions. When she gains control of herself, try and allow her to put the body into perspective.'

This analysis has something in common with John Russell Brown's account of how William Gaskill carefully prepared for, and Vanessa Redgrave skilfully executed, Innogen's only gradual consciousness of her situation. But the effect was clearer in Phillips's analysis than in his production. Martha Burns is no Vanessa Redgrave, and she was unable to establish a convincing rhythm for the speech. She moved about too much and so fragmented the speech rather than gradually building from the controlled beginning that Phillips wanted to the climax; but when, at the end, she put her leg over the 'Martial thigh' she took to be Posthumus's, the weird necrophilic embrace recalled Giacomo's physical intimacy with her in the bedroom.

If the full sense of a nightmare experience was not achieved in this scene as it had been in the bedroom, it was certainly fully recaptured in the Jupiter scene, which was presented with a theatrical 'call to attention' like Giacomo's throat microphone, but far exceeding it in sensational effect, as is appropriate to the episode. The Jupiter scene was the climax of a precisely calculated dramatic sequence based firmly on the experiences of Posthumus. The production recovered spectacularly from the trough into which it had fallen in the burial scene. It could build upon the very strong impact made by all the scenes involving Giacomo or Posthumus or both, and especially upon the realism of those scenes. Indeed, theatrical virtuosity and psychological realism were combined in this sequence so that it emerged as the most revealing in the production. Constantly changing shafts of light picked out the characters at crucial moments. When the Roman army in their trenchcoats marched across the stage, one of the soldiers turned back to light a cigarette, his face suddenly caught in a shaft of light: in this way Giacomo's presence was instantly re-established. The thrust stage itself became the 'narrow lane' in which Posthumus, Belarius, and the princes, picked out by very located lighting, repelled wave after wave of Italian troops. The virtuosity of the staging resembled that of William Gaskill's production at the other Stratford, except that it was a much more ferocious battle, in keeping with the director's unusual stress upon the importance and seriousness of the war in the play.

That very ferocity went a long way towards explaining why Shakespeare asks for the battle to be acted out and then provides Posthumus with a long and vivid account of it. Phillips himself began by evading this problem rather than confronting it. He initially divided the speech up among other members of the company, as if they were nurses writing home, or journalists sending copy to their newspapers. But just before the production opened, he restored the speech to Posthumus. Robert Gaines reports that Joseph Ziegler, playing Posthumus, felt that 'the "arc the character has to complete in the second half of the play somehow lacked that completeness" until he began doing the speech' (p. 281). In other words, Shakespeare knows what he is doing, and Ziegler suggested what that was. Instead of being a redundant description of something the audience has already seen for themselves, it became another theatrical *tour de force*. Ziegler delivered it with a sophisticated virtuosity which brought out the underlying emotional reality: Posthumus was badly shell-shocked, as shaken by the violence of war as he had earlier been by his uncertainty about Innogen. There was a direct connection between the violence outside him and that inside; going through the battle was a terrifying experience but also a therapeutic one, releasing and for the time being exhausting that inner violence. This interpretation corresponded well with the ferocious imagery of the speech, in which soldiers 'grin like lions / Upon the pikes o' th' hunters' (V.v.38-9). The character grew up before our eyes, maturing from a callow youth to a man chastened by grim experience.

The Jupiter scene followed naturally from this: it became the exhausted dream of someone who had just endured a violent battle. Phillips determined to present a modern spectacle as full of shock value as the baroque extravagance of the descending god, and he clearly understood Shakespeare's motive for using such a device, to 'alert' the audience and to 'startle them awake for the Fifth Act' (Gaines, p. 282). He certainly achieved his aim. The doggerel of the apparitions was overlapped so that is sounded like the confused, incoherent babble of a nightmare. At its climax, Jupiter suddenly materialised on the balcony, as he had done in Jean Gascon's production; but this was a very different *deus ex machina* from Gascon's, and literally *ex machina*: 'eagle' appeared to be the name of a Second World War bomber, a 'thunderer' whose huge propellers revolved just below the balcony. Immediately above them, Jupiter was the pilot in his cockpit, whose 'bolt, . . . / Sky-planted, batters all rebelling coasts' (V.v.189-90) – that is, he would bomb them into submission. Jupiter roared his ferocious message into a microphone (his 'radio') in front of him. The extreme sensationalism of this staging perhaps ran the risk of distracting from the lines, but Shakespeare runs that risk himself by using the eagle, and by providing a modern spectacle to match or out-do Shakespeare's own, Philips clarified the nature and purpose of the scene. Much of Jupiter's language is in fact violent; he is a dangerous as well as a benevolent deity. He promises that Posthumus

> shall be lord of Lady Innogen,
> And happier much by his affliction made (V.v.201-2)

but it is important that to achieve this greater happiness, Posthumus, like Innogen, must endure 'affliction'.

The public military violence of the bomber made perfect sense in terms of Posthumus's dream, since it was not only the logical climax of the military action he had seen, but also connected in his mind with the private violence towards Innogen which was on his conscience, of which he therefore dreamed, and from which he hoped to be freed, as Jupiter promises he will. This particular vision focused attention on the maturing Posthumus in a way that few productions have done because it was so obviously an externalisation of his dream and an expression of his shaken mental state. It was, in short, exactly the 'therapeutic dream' that Moshinsky calls it but which his version fails to suggest because it does not rise to the theatrical virtuosity of the scene. This is not a scene for half-measures. It demands as vivid a theatrical spectacle as possible; only then will it carry out its function of alerting, even shocking the audience into concentrating on Posthumus's state. By placing Posthumus in exactly the same place on the stage as Innogen by Cloten's corpse, in the same ghostly light, Phillips stressed that husband and wife had to undergo the same traumatic purgative experiences.

For the final scene, the stage was transformed with lightning suddenness into a field hospital, with wounded soldiers lying in every part of the huge stage, which was dominated by a gigantic cannon, in whose threatening presence the reunions took place. Its function was clearly to suggest the fragile, tentative nature of the peace which the text celebrates. This had advantages and disadvantages. It legitimately emphasised how violence keeps surfacing in the scene: in Cymbeline's threat to kill the Roman prisoners, in his animosity to Belarius, and especially when Posthumus strikes Innogen. Of this, Phillips says: 'After what the characters have been through to rid themselves of the aggression of war, notice how quickly aggressive acts erupt again' (Gaines, p. 284). Gaines reports that Martha Burns felt that the reunion was, for this reason, a precarious one, that she and Posthumus are 'damaged people', and that they achieve a 'real' rather than a 'happy' ending (p. 284). These two kinds of ending are not necessarily antithetical, as she implies, but their reunion was both real and moving. Their silent, chastened response to each other during the multiple revelations going on all around them was convincing precisely because the rigours they had undergone had been so graphically staged. Nor was the ending wholly dark: Innogen's reunion with her brothers involved laughter at their recollection of those comradely blows they had exchanged earlier on. But in general it was an appropriate ending to a serious, dark reading rather than one which dwelt on the lyrical beauty of the play.

Although Phillips wanted the cannon to introduce 'a destructive element' into the reconciliations, the scene in performance may have seemed more uncompromising than he actually intended. He had originally wanted that cannon to be 'swallowed up by nature, with weeds growing over it. The final image on stage, without the weeds, was "incomplete" to him' (Gaines, pp. 282-3) because he believed that in the play man tries to keep out the natural world, 'But nature replies, "No, you can't. I am stronger than anything man-made"' (Gaines, pp. 259-60). This might appear to be a legitimate response to the play's constant evocation of the natural world; had they been there, those weeds covering the cannon might have connected with Arviragus's image of the furred moss covering a human body. On the other hand, Phillips cannot be said to have tried very hard to communicate the influence of nature upon human action. He cut those lines of Arviragus's; he staged the burial scene in a very contrived way; and, like his predecessor on this stage, he sent up 'Hark, hark, the lark' with his own special brand of triviality: it was a 'ricky-ticky version sung by a Rudy Valee-type crooner' emerging from a wind-up gramophone (Gaines, p. 264). This was an example of the danger of too rigorously detailed an updating: the audience's attention is drawn to the director's ingenuity in making the text fit the new period rather than to the qualities of the text itself. The danger of overwhelming the play with an excess of invention partly explains why the rural scenes worked less well than in, for instance, the previous Ontario production. Simplicity is of the essence in these scenes, and simplicity does not come easily to Phillips.

He was, nevertheless, aware of such qualities in the play. He describes the language as having 'a more accessible verse structure' that 'sits on the tongue more colloquially than in many of [Shakespeare's] other plays. . . . It's still verse but it is getting closer and closer to naturalistic speech.' This 'accessible' language made its greatest effect where it fitted the sophisticated realism of the production, in the wager plot rather than in the rural one. In general, Phillips encouraged a noticeably less flamboyant delivery than Gascon. In his final comment on the play, Phillips called it both 'theatrical and traumatic. . . . The humanity is so vital, you find it unbelievable the play is not done more often.' Here Phillips puts his finger on what really matters in this play: it is both 'theatrical' *and* 'traumatic'; he clearly doesn't see any contradiction between theatricality and 'humanity'. And his production decisively underlined this, reinforcing the evidence provided by Gaskill and Gascon that the theatricality of the play is a way of arresting the audience's attention for a revelation of extreme emotional states, or 'traumas', as he follows Moshinsky in calling them.

I   Peggy Ashcroft as Innogen, Stratford-upon-Avon, 1957. (Photo: Angus McBean)

II   The descent of Jupiter (John Corvin), Stratford-upon-Avon, 1962. (Photo: Gordon Goode)

III   The battle scene, Stratford-upon-Avon, 1962. Arviragus (Barry MacGregor), Guiderius (Brian Murray), Posthumus (Patrick Allen, *above*), Caius Lucius (Tony Steedman). (Photo: Gordon Goode)

IV   Posthumus (Patrick Allen) strikes Innogen (Vanessa Redgrave) in the final scene, Stratford-upon-Avon, 1962. *Background, left*: Guiderius (Brian Murray), Cymbeline (Tom Fleming), Belarius (Paul Hardwick). *Background, right*: Giacomo (Eric Porter). (Photo: Gordon Goode)

V   Giacomo (Colm Feore) proposes the wager to Posthumus (Joseph Ziegler) in an Italian gentlemen's club in the 1930s. Stratford, Ontario, 1986. (Photo: Robert C. Ragsdale)

VI   Giacomo (Donald Sumpter) proposes the wager to Posthumus (Nicholas Farrell). The Other Place, Stratford-upon-Avon, 1987. (Photo: Joe Cocks Studio)

Innogen and Posthumus endure their purgations, National Theatre, 1988. (Photos: John Haynes)

VII   Innogen (Geraldine James) embracing Cloten's corpse.

VIII   Posthumous (Peter Woodward) beneath the emblematic heavens designed by Alison Chitty.

Photos I-IV are from the Shakespeare Centre Library, Stratford-upon-Avon. Photo VI is from the Shakespearian Festival Foundation of Canada. All photographs are reproduced by permission.

III

IV

V

VI

VIII

VII

CHAPTER VI

Small-scale *Cymbeline:*
Bill Alexander's production,
Stratford-upon-Avon, 1987

Robin Phillips's elaborately theatrical realism in Ontario contrasted sharply with Bill Alexander's very different brand of
realism the following year in the intimacy of The Other Place,
Stratford-upon-Avon. This is the Royal Shakespeare Company's
studio theatre, little more than a corrugated iron hut. Performances in this space are necessarily on a small scale, and in this
case Bill Alexander went out of his way to present the play with
the minimum of staging. He told the story directly and realistic-
ally, with the emphasis on powerful emotions, and with any aspect
of staging that might distract from the individual performances
severely cut back.

There was not even a suggestion of a set, merely some sloping
black diagonal lines on the back wall which carried the faint hint
of eagle's wings. Props and costumes were obviously intended to
draw as little attention to themselves as possible. The few pieces
of furniture used – a few tables and chairs, the Queen's medicine
cabinet, Innogen's bed – were very plain, and the costumes were
basic and unostentatious: sober doublets and brown trousers
tucked into boots for the men, very simple dresses of no particular
period for the women. Innogen was almost an Alice-in-Wonderland
figure with her waist-length hair and gold circlet. The closest the
production came to 'costuming' was in Cymbeline's black fur robe
(his crown was a simple coronet) and in the smart red waistcoat

that Giacomo wore beneath his leather doublet. This momentarily suggested a villain from Victorian melodrama, but any such associations were swiftly banished by the subtle interpretation of Giacomo that in fact emerged. Because the period was so unspecific, the clash of periods in the text raised no problems: there was nothing classically Roman about Caius Lucius, for instance, whose red leather doublet was barely distinguishable from Giacomo's.

Since there was no room for a set in The Other Place in any case, Bill Alexander was spared the problem of having to decide whether the action was to take place in mythical, Renaissance, or modern times. The Other Place was just a room in which to tell a story, with the audience grouped on three sides of a very small acting area. But the performance was not confined to this area. Cymbeline battered on the outer door of The Other Place in his furious eagerness to get at the lovers and part them; several scenes were prefaced by the sound of Cymbeline or the Queen calling Innogen from outside. This gave the impression of a claustrophobic court in which Innogen was virtually a prisoner, and it also had the effect of involving the audience in her plight, since they were shut inside The Other Place with her while sinister cries penetrated from outside.

The audience were also lured into the action by the staging of the opening scene. The two gentlemen sat opposite one another in the front row of the audience. As in earlier productions, the actor of Cornelius also played the First Gentleman and the Lord who mocks Cloten. In a tense, whispered exchange with the other gentleman, he swiftly sketched in the basic situation, confiding individual phrases to members of the audience, as he also did the asides in the Cloten scenes. In this context, direct address to the audience caused even fewer problems than usual, not only in soliloquies like Belarius's life-story or Innogen's account of her weariness in III.vi, but also in the middle of conversation: Giacomo did not need to move from the centre of the stage to confide to this audience 'All of her that is out of door most rich!' (I.vi.15) as Innogen turned away to read her letter.

Music, usually a combination of humming and tubular bells, was also used with restraint, mostly to emphasise the folk-tale elements, as in the reference to the theft of the princes twenty years previously. The production's emphasis on telling a story could have led very easily into stressing that it was *just* a story';

it could have paraded the play's 'theatrical self-consciousness' in order to distance the events and send them up, but this the company resolutely refused to do. The intimate relationship they established with the audience made it very easy to draw laughter, but they did so only very sparingly and where the text positively asks for it, principally in the Cloten scenes. This company clearly had great faith in the play, which they presented almost uncut, and took its events absolutely seriously. Indeed, the production suggested that to concentrate upon story-telling actually requires the cast to take the emotions seriously rather than distancing them. The paradox at the heart of this version was that a staging on such a small scale should also have presented the human passions with such intensity, often to explosion point and accompanied by extreme physical violence.

The Innogen/Posthumus relationship, for instance, was much more overtly sexual than in other productions: they clung passionately to each other in the first scene; their parting kiss was prolonged and intense. Innogen's

> Nay, stay a little.
> Were you but riding forth to air yourself
> Such parting were too petty (I.i.110-12)

was desperate, almost frenzied. These were not lovers from remote romance but very much creatures of flesh and blood. But their passion did not require a generalised 'emotional' treatment of the lines. Indeed, it was characteristic of the production's reconsideration of every detail of the text that Posthumus's 'How another' (I.i.115) was not an exclamation as usual – 'How, another!' – but a logical question: 'In what way could I love another?' The impassioned treatment extended to the Innogen/Cymbeline argument. Beside himself with rage, Cymbeline struck her in the face at 'hence from my sight!' (I.i.126) before turning on Posthumus; momentarily stunned, she soon responded with a furious counter-accusation, 'Sir, / It is *your fault* that I have loved Posthumus' (I.i.144-5), demonstrating how Innogen is equipped with what Michael Bawtree in the 1970 Ontario programme called 'a temper of devastating openness'. She was certainly her father's daughter. So frenzied was their exchange that as early as the fifth performance there was some danger of it degenerating into a mere slanging match – but it unquestionably established the production's uncompromising point of view: there was nothing to laugh at in these extreme events. This did not mean, however, that Innogen lacked a wry sense of humour, which first emerged at the mention of Cloten's attack upon Posthumus:

> I would they were in Afric both together,
> Myself by with a needle, that I might prick
> The goer-back. (I.i.168-70)

As James Sutherland remarks in his illuminating article on the language of the last plays, 'the idea of Innogen dancing round the angry swordsmen pricking with her needle the buttocks of the retreating Cloten is a highly recondite one' (in John Garrett, ed., *More Talking of Shakespeare*, 1959, pp. 156-7). The point was not lost in Harriet Walter's performance. In this first scene, she quickly established the mercurial variety of the part.

At this tyrannical court, Innogen and Pisanio had to meet in secret, snatching a few moments together by the light of a candle to have a whispered conversation about Posthumus's departure. Confining the light and space threw all attention upon the language; the tightly enclosed staging drew especial attention to the way in which the style itself often contracts, focusing upon something very small in order to express intense feeling, particularly intense pain, as in Innogen's

> I would have broke mine eye-strings, cracked them, but
> To look upon him till the diminution
> Of space had pointed him sharp as my needle;
> Nay, followed him till he had melted from
> The smallness of a gnat to air, and then
> Have turned mine eye and wept. (I.iii.17-22)

Since the staging precisely matched the process described here ('the diminution / Of space'), it brought out the way in which this particular speech is written, and Harriet Walter expressed Innogen's despair by miming with gesturing fingers the vanishing of Posthumus like a gnat disappearing to nothingness.

In the wager scene, too, light coming principally from a single source focused upon a small area of the stage: an overhead lamp illuminating an Italian café table served to spotlight every reaction of Giacomo and Posthumus, however slight, and to concentrate on their very quiet, insistent, tense delivery of the text. In this intimate space, the production was able to carry to a new extreme the naturalistic delivery adopted by Robin Phillips's version in Ontario the year before. Phillips pointed out how many scenes in

Cymbeline 'have the upper echelons of the cast speaking in what amounts to prose', and much of the verse in this production sounded like tense, urgent prose. The wager scene is of course actually in prose, and the quietly riveting performances of Giacomo and Posthumus demonstrated the advantages of the approach. Like Colm Feore's in Ontario the previous year, Donald Sumpter's Giacomo was partly a representative of a hedonistic society who openly mocked Posthumus's idealism: this Giacomo cupped an Italian lady's breasts in each hand to point the line 'as fair and as good – a kind of hand-in-hand comparison' (I.iv. 68–9); but, also like Feore, something dangerous was contained within the easy-going manner. Where he differed from Feore was that there was no hint of the psychotic: it was not Giacomo but Posthumus who made the running in their quarrel.

Nicholas Farrell as Posthumus used a softly spoken, dulcet delivery to suggest the romantic lover, but the honeyed manner concealed a basic insecurity that kept surfacing in moments of teeth-clenching tension and in sudden, alarming outbursts. From the very start of the wager scene, his behaviour was provocative: here was a man who was very touchy indeed about other people's reactions to his wife. This was immediately evident in his icy response to the Frenchman's admittedly mocking reference to Innogen's reputation as a 'slight and trivial' motive for a quarrel: Posthumus's tone was steely beneath the apparent modesty of 'if I *offend not* to say it [his judgment] is mended', and the next line – 'my quarrel was not altogether slight' – was an edged rebuke (I.iv.41-7). As the scene proceeded, the dulcet manner itself began to seem provocative, for example in the understated but supercilious 'She holds her virtue still, and I my mind' (I.iv.63). He froze the atmosphere very rapidly, understandably provoking a correspondingly edged reaction from Giacomo, which led to the wager. Posthumus's response was counter-attack: as he said 'I fear not my ring', he flaunted it on his finger, and when Giacomo said that he would 'get ground' of Innogen, Posthumus delivered 'no, no' with a dismissive laugh. This Posthumus was certainly inviting trouble: 'You bear a graver purpose, I hope' (I.iv.136-7) was an overt challenge to Giacomo to carry out the wager, and the scene ended with the two of them confronting each other across that table.

Donald Sumpter's genial, open manner was a great advantage in making his attempted seduction of Innogen seem plausible.

Again, the tightly confined space and the very quiet delivery exposed their interplay to intense scrutiny. Sumpter pitched the volume at such a low – but always audible – level that it was entirely credible that 'What, are men mad?' and the following speeches (I.vi.33-52) should appear to be scarcely more than thoughts spoken aloud by a preoccupied Giacomo, and only half caught by Innogen. The *sotto voce* level was also most effective for the hints, innuendoes, and carefully timed pauses that followed, recalling in this respect the Eric Porter/Vanessa Redgrave exchange in Gaskill's version:

> *Giacomo.* (*hinting*)   But heavens know
>   Some men are much to blame.
> *Innogen.* (*very quiet, tense*) Not he, I hope.
> *Giacomo.* (*equally quiet*) Not he; (*pause*) but yet heaven's bounty
>   towards him might
>   Be used more thankfully. (I.vi.77-80)

Innogen was initially sceptical about his account of Posthumus's behavour: 'Will my lord say so?' (I.vi. 74) was suspicious, almost sulky; but he seemed so sympathetic to her, so concerned about Posthumus's apparent misbehaviour, that she was soon urging him with all the passion she had displayed in earlier scenes to tell her the truth. 'My lord, I fear, / Has forgot Britain' (I.vi.113-14) was a direct challenge to his veracity; they faced one another, eye to eye, in what looked like a deliberate echo of the Giacomo/Posthumus confrontation at the end of the wager scene; and it is worth comparing this with Moshinsky's television handling of the Giacomo/Innogen scene, where there is also an eye-to-eye challenge to veracity: it is surely far more convincing that Innogen should challenge Giacomo than that he should challenge her, as on television.

Sumpter delivered the description of Posthumus's supposed whores, 'such boiled stuff / As well might poison poison' (I.vi.126-7), with his customary quiet concern, so that he could slip easily and plausibly into the contrast between Posthumus 'vaulting variable ramps' and his own quiet dedication of himself to her sweet pleasure (ll. 135-7). This sometimes seems a clumsy ploy; here it seemed a skilful piece of sexual manipulation; nevertheless Harriet Walter saw through it, and laughed out loud in relief as she said 'Away!'. This laughter cued Giacomo's own, as he retracted his slanders, a retraction made the more plausible by the return of his earlier genial manner. As he claimed that he had merely been testing her, she bit her lip as if to say 'How could I have been such a fool?' She was in fact no fool, but an intelligent girl whose relieved laughter eased the tension and therefore made the next development equally convincing. Casually, hands in pockets, he introduced the topic of the trunk. She was not given the slightest cause for suspicion; relieved, freed from fear, she allowed her generous temperament full rein and responded to his geniality with complete trust. Harriet Walter is a serious actress with rather dour facial expressions, who is slow to melt; but when she does so, the effect is delightful, like the sun coming out. That was how she played 'I thank you for your pains' (I.vi.204), laughingly embarrassed at having caused him trouble, and genuinely wanting him to stay: 'But not away tomorrow!' Giacomo caught her tone in his reply 'O, I must, madam' (I.vi.205), and the scene ended with the niceties of relaxed social conversation, making the situation all the more dangerous for that reason.

The bedroom scene was a particular success because it was able to build upon the production and performance style so securely established by this point. Like the earlier scenes, it was staged with the utmost simplicity. A plain, unadorned bed was placed beside a candle at the front of the acting area, almost surrounded by members of the audience. The trunk was upstage. The humming sound used in the music elsewhere recurred, and the lady-in-waiting hummed as well, as if singing her mistress to sleep. A very great tension was established, prolonged by silence before the trunk lid slowly opened. Giacomo stole out, and his bare feet touched a squeaky board on the Other Place floor: he froze nervously, then slipped into a chair among the audience; this at once increased the tension and lured the audience further into the action. The very quiet delivery earlier now paid double dividends. We were used to it, especially from this Giacomo, and used also to paying hushed attention to what was being expressed. As he kissed her, she stirred and almost woke, intensifying the tension for the crucial moment of the scene. She wore a simple nightgown, buttoned down the front. In order to discover 'some natural notes about her body' (II.ii. 28), he gently undid the top buttons, so that he was able to see the mole *under*, not just upon, her breast. The text was altered to correspond with the more specific reference to the position of the mole at II.iv. 134-5, and such precision was very typical of this painstaking production. Then came the possibility of rape. He undid some lower buttons, but changed his mind – 'No more' (II.ii.42) – and the danger passed. This very simple but very convincing moment was entirely characteristic of this performance: the potential of the scene was fully realised without turning the character into either a voyeur or a sadist, and was expressed very simply without requiring the elaborate theatricality of Phillips's Ontario staging. As he returned to the trunk the clock struck three times, as the text suggests: there was no need for it to strike during the scene to increase tension, since the claustrophobic intimacy and the quiet, intense delivery were sufficient in themselves.

Quiet intensity was also the keynote of the second Giacomo/Posthumus scene, which had even more impact than the first: the effect was cumulative. Again, an overhead light focused upon a table, this time a green baize card table, possibly to underline, like the chessboard in the television version, the sense of people manoeuvring each other. The atmosphere was uneasy from the start, Filario as well as Posthumus appearing apprehensive. When Giacomo arrived, he and Posthumus initially confronted one another as they had done at the end of their previous scene. There was none of the elaborate preparation of Robin Phillips's version, with its contrasting of a literally laid-back Giacomo and a nervous Posthumus. Instantly Posthumus took the offensive, brandishing the ring on 'Sparkles this stone as it was wont?' (II.iv.40), and exploding with rage both on 'The stone's too hard to come by' and on 'Make not, sir, / Your loss your sport' (II.iv.46, 47-8). Giacomo, seated at the card table, made the most of his mockery of the 'winking Cupids' in Innogen's bedroom, but still without raising his voice; this provided maximum contrast with Posthumus's violent banging on the table at 'This is her honour!' (II.iv.89-91). Here, Nicholas Farrell contrasted not only with this Giacomo but also with the smiling irony that Michael Pennington brought to this line in the television version. Farrell's Posthumus was a man who seemed to be asking for his worst fears to be confirmed.

After Giacomo had given him a quick glimpse of the bracelet, which he wore on his arm, Posthumus's 'Is it that / Which I left with her?' (II.iv.99-100) played straight into Giacomo's hands, giving him fresh information which he was quick to use. Realising that the bracelet was of special significance, he flaunted it as Posthumus had the ring, and the quietly taunting question 'She writes so to you, doth she?', which in most performances emerges as a cool contrast with a showier delivery of Giacomo's other speeches, was here very much of a piece with Sumpter's playing of the whole scene: he hardly needed to persuade Posthumus further. 'No, no' was long drawn out, in anguish; Posthumus was shattered, but in a way he wanted to believe what Giacomo told him. The point was underlined by Filario's reasoned intervention, for this Posthumus even seized *him* in his frenzy, and his passion reached new heights on a bawled 'Never talk on't. / She hath been *colted* by him' (II.iv.132-3), though he did not attempt the feature-distorting grimaces that Michael Pennington used to express the grossness of Posthumus's imaginings. At 'No swearing' (II.iv.143), he physically assaulted Giacomo, who became increasingly amazed at the tempest he had unleashed inside Posthumus – but witnessing Posthumus's excesses made him feel guilty about his deceit: this was written all over his face. His final 'With all my heart' was as quiet as the rest of his performance, but this time the quietness expressed the beginnings of the repentance he shows when he reappears in Act V. It was beautifully prepared for. Posthumus's soliloquy prepared less well for his reappearance. The preceding scene was played at so fevered a pitch that the soliloquy had nowhere else to go, and Farrell missed the modulations of tone in a disappointingly unvaried rendering.

There was nothing either disappointing or unvaried about Innogen's handling of the two scenes which are a consequence of that soliloquy. Harriet Walter played the first of them, when Innogen plans the journey to Milford Haven, with a kind of muted ecstasy in keeping with the small-scale approach. She was able to draw on the relieved happiness which she had expressed with a winning smile at the end of her scene with Giacomo; it was as if another load was lifted from her shoulders – though of course this is another delusion, and her excited delivery of

> Why, one that rode to's execution, man,
> Could never go so slow (III.ii.70-1)

pointed the irony. That was characteristic of the production's sharp focus upon verbal detail, and an even more telling example occurred in the next lines:

> I have heard of riding wagers
> Where horses have been nimbler than the sands
> That run i' th' clock's behalf. (III.ii.71-3)

Most productions omit these lines. They may seem to be an example of what Frank Kermode in his *TLS* review of John Barton's production calls Shakespeare's 'garrulities' in this play, but as Kermode goes on to say, the cutting of such apparent 'superfluities . . . in a measure falsifies the play'. When they are included, their function becomes clear. Shakespeare is once again drawing on the animal world for a vivid image which sharply expresses what the character is feeling, and it refers back to her cry 'O for a horse with wings!' earlier in the scene (III.ii.48). Reviewing Vanessa Redgrave's performance, when the passage was also given complete, John Russell Brown pointed out the effect of these references to horses, 'a sweeping fancy that travels on a winged horse more nimbly than the sands in an hour glass', adding that Vanessa Redgrave's rendering 'did not swerve from a lightly urgent raptness' (*Shakespeare Survey 16*, p. 146). Harriet Walter's smaller-scale treatment was more detailed, using the image to point the character's excitement and new-found happiness, and also giving the impression of the release of those strong passions that had had to be communicated by frustration in the opening scenes. It was enchantingly done, as moving as Vanessa Redgrave had been, in a quite different style. And it made her disillusion with Posthumus in her next scene doubly effective.

When she came to the word 'strumpet' as she read Posthumus's letter (III.iv.22), there followed a long pause of disbelief before the cruel truth sank in. Her indignation was then expressed as passionately as her love had been: 'I false!' (III.iv.46) was not heart-broken; she was absolutely furious with Posthumus. 'Why, I *must* die' (l. 74) was equally impassioned, and led to a physical struggle with Pisanio as she tried to get hold of his sword. Even Pisanio displayed the passion, expressed in physical terms, that was such a feature of the production. When Innogen angrily cried that she had been betrayed by 'some Roman courtesan', Pisanio seized her at 'No, on my life!' as if to shake some sense into her – and then had to bow apologetically to her for doing so (III.iv.123-4).

This Pisanio was a great help to this Innogen. He was played much younger than usual, so that Cloten had to omit 'old' from the phrase 'Pisanio, her old servant' (III.v. 54). If this was a distortion of the text, it was entirely justified by the gains that resulted. Here was a young, inexperienced servant who was left by his employer to cope with a series of extremely difficult situations. He grew up very fast as he improvised solutions – and his integrity and goodness emerged increasingly as he measured up to the magnitude of his task, rather than simply being 'given' from the start. His youth made the alliance with his young mistress from their whispered conversation in I.iii seem very natural. Actresses often remark that they spend far more time on stage with Pisanio than with Posthumus: in this production Harriet Walter and Jim Hooper touchingly suggested two inexperienced people deriving mutual strength from one another as they faced adversity together. This was very much in line with the production's emphasis upon human feeling, and provided a fine moment to end the scene and the first half of the production. Pisanio retrieved the letters from Posthumus which Innogen had thrown angrily away, and handed them back to her as if to urge her not to lose faith in his master. She looked resentfully at them, but then accepted both the letters and Pisanio's compassionate loyalty with 'I thank thee' (III.iv.194) This young Pisanio, growing up before our eyes, represented a reversal of the standard way of playing this part as a reliable embodiment of constancy 'not to be shaked' (I.v.76), and demonstrated the variety of interpretation to which even the most apparently straightforward roles in Shakespeare are open.

In general, the 'main' plot here was as effective as I have seen it. Other parts of the play, however, including the Welsh scenes, were more uncertain in impact; and this uncertainty was reflected in Bruce Alexander's Cloten, an uneasy performance of a character who connects somewhat uneasily with each plot. His scenes with the lords were played very broadly indeed, as a comic underplot divorced from the main action, perhaps to allow the audience a release from the tension demanded of them by the unremitting intensity of the wager plot. But then the serenade scene (II.iii.) came as a great surprise. Cloten unexpectedly sang 'Hark, hark, the lark' himself, delightfully, and only sent it up as he snapped out of the song with a curtly dismissive 'So, get you gone' to the musicians. When Cymbeline and the Queen appeared, however, he seemed to become – or possibly to be enacting the role of – a naughty boy, chidden by his mother. And then his image changed again, to a man capable of *conscious* word play:

> I will make
> One of her women lawyer to me, for
> I yet *not understand* the case myself (II.iii.71-3)

was a deliberate joke on his part. But this witty, musical personality was at odds with the naughty boy and the clod. Possibly the intention was to reflect the variety of the writing and the unpredictability of the character, but the various 'faces' of the role did not come together in a coherent characterisation as they did in some previous Clotens.

The one link between the early Cloten scenes and the wager plot was that Cloten's arbitrary outbursts – his 'bursts of speaking' – were as furious, psychotic even, as Posthumus's own; and the exchange between Innogen and Cloten at the end of the serenade scene was certainly a parody of the parting of Innogen and Posthumus. Harriet Walter brought to it not only the passion but also the humour and the verbal detail from her other scenes. For instance, her

> I care not for you,
> And am so near the lack of charity
> To accuse myself I hate you (II.iii.105-7)

was spoken in a reasonable, logical manner which nevertheless expressed her frustration and was also very funny. But the exchange turned nasty at the end. When 'bursts of speaking' failed, Cloten seized her ferociously at 'I'll be revenged' (II.iii.152) in a parody of Posthumus's passionate embrace at the start. She was momentarily shocked and alarmed, but then she simply laughed at him, broke away, and left him 'to th' worst of discontent'. The total impression given by Cloten was uncertain rather than complex, lacking the incisiveness of the Innogen/Giacomo/Posthumus scenes.

The small-scale treatment made a whole area of the play hard to bring off. The political meeting between Cymbeline and Caius Lucius needs a sense of occasion that was necessarily absent in this restricted space. More surprisingly, the production failed to find a natural rhythm for the Welsh scenes. The princes wore ragged versions of what the other characters were wearing, Belarius rusty chain mail beneath a rough robe trimmed with fur. His manner was oddly eccentric with his staring eyes and wild white hair. Yet there was no attempt, as this might suggest, to send up these characters. In the absence of a set, they stooped as they arrived on stage, miming the entrance to the cave. The two princes were differentiated by their delivery of 'Hail, heaven!': Arviragus was gushing and mannered, Guiderius a muttering Glaswegian yob. Like their eccentric 'father', they missed the all-important simplicity of the scenes. The production seemed to be trying too hard to 'interpret' the scenes, and to relate them to the wager plot. The princes were as passionate in their resentment at being made to live in a cave as the lovers had been in their embraces; Belarius responded in kind, grabbing them both by the scruff of the neck and pinning them to the ground for answering back. The effect was forced, whereas the passsion of the lovers was quite spontaneous. For the first time in the performance, the director seemed uneasy with the material.

These scenes improved with the arrival of Innogen. Like Judi Dench at Stratford in 1979, Harriet Walter made the most of the moments of humour in her male disguise, notably at 'Two beggars told me / I could not miss my way' (III.vi.8-9), as people always do when you ask them for directions. And her rapidly thrown off

> Best draw my sword, and if mine enemy
> But fear the sword like me he'll scarcely look on't (III.vi.25-6)

was very funny, without sacrificing the pathos of her predicament. The stolidness of Guiderius, a drawback for much of the time, was an advantage in the encounter with Cloten: he simply stood there imperturbably, as immovable as a rock or a tree against which Cloten spent his fury in vain. Finally Guiderius merely picked him up and carried him offstage. But it seemed odd for Belarius to praise the royalty of such princes. There was a clash between what was said and how it was presented that never occurred in the Giacomo scenes.

This uncertainty carried through into the burial scene. The humming and tubular bells sounded again to suggest the 'ingenious instrument' and to underpin 'With fairest flowers' and the dirge, as if the director didn't trust them to work unaided. Yet Arviragus's 'The bird is dead' worked its usual magic as he appeared with Innogen in his arms: the audience craned forward tensely, clearly involved in the moment. The dirge was no fluently spoken set piece, but a heartfelt attempt by rather inarticulate people to express their grief and love. 'Golden lads' was made to refer specifically to Innogen/Fidele; 'come to dust' was very emphatic, as if they were trying to come to terms with the fact by dwelling upon it. The consoling phrases were emotionally laboured. The whole effect was forced, missing the simplicity and naturalness of the lines, so that these princes failed to involve us in their grief for someone whom they had loved and lost – which is to miss the point of the scene.

The scene recovered its grip with Innogen's awakening, when Harriet Walter took control and swiftly demonstrated that she had the measure of the speech. As she gradually became aware of her predicament with a sharply edged 'This bloody man the care on't' (IV.ii.299), she recoiled from the body. The severed head had drawn a few nervous giggles; the bloody neck was covered by a hood, partly so as to avoid the risk of giggles in the early part of the scene, but also so that Innogen's discovery could come as a greater shock to her. Tentatively, she approached the hood, pulled it away, and hastily replaced it with horrified realisation: 'A headless man!' This gave way to the appalling certainty of her identification of the body. 'Damned Pisanio' was not an exclamation but spoken suddenly and rapidly as a direct accusation. She buried her face in the neck at the lines 'O Posthumus, alas, / Where is thy head?', and the pathos completely avoided any danger of laughter. It was only narrowly avoided, however, when she followed the Oxford Shakespeare's stage direction, dipped her fingers into the blood, and smeared her face with it. This was the more unnecessary here since she could easily have bloodied her face during her passionate embrace, as Vanessa Redgrave did.

The public world intruded upon Innogen's private grief in the form of deafening drum-beats as Caius Lucius arrived on stage. This effectively made the point that violence involving individuals gives way to public, military violence. And this transition from the personal to the public anticipated a similar process at the end of the play, when a peace that is made between individuals blossoms into a peace between nations. Harriet Walter's bloodstained face and characteristically mournful expression vividly underlined the traumatic experience she had been through, and she caught all the pathos of 'I am nothing' and the subsequent speeches, especially since this final part of the scene was given in full. This meant that Caius Lucius for once had all his lines with which to express his compassion for her. A telling detail was that his promise to find 'the prettiest daisied plot we can' for the grave (IV.ii.399) was not a straightforward description but a phrase designed to comfort Innogen: as so often in the text, a reference to the natural world was used to express human feeling. So assured was the grip of the scene, with the audience again leaning tensely forward, that there were no laughs either during the soliloquy or at Caius Lucius's 'what trunk is here / Without his top?' (IV.ii.355-6) which can be a dangerous moment. The chief reason for the success of this episode was that it was possible to present it to maximum effect within the terms of the general approach. The intimacy, the quiet tone, and the stress on verbal detail focused upon human emotion presented in extreme form.

It was harder to do this in the following scenes. When Posthumus reappeared, however, the intense scrutiny of the text encouraged by the close focus brought out an interesting point that I had not noticed in other performances. The touches of cynicism at the end of Posthumus's angry soliloquy in II.v. recur in the opening lines of the repentant one, so that the two speeches relate to one another:

> You married ones,
> If each of you should take this course, how many
> Must murder wives much better than themselves
> For wrying but a little! (V.i.2-5)

Shakespeare is taking Posthumus from one extreme emotion to another, but he uses the same cynical habit of mind in order to do so. But if the small-scale approach helped to make that clear, this sequence as a whole, from V.i. to the Jupiter scene, defined the limitations of a chamber approach. The battle and Jupiter scenes need space and spectacle for their full impact, and the director's ingenuity could not provide those. When Posthumus resolved

> I'll disrobe me
> Of these Italian weeds, and suit myself
> As does a Briton peasant (V.i.22-4)

he took off both doublet and shirt, but this method of disguise made little sense because the princes had not established naked-ness as the norm for a 'Briton peasant', as their counterparts did in Jean Gascon's Ontario version. This inconsistency was emphasised when Posthumus marched side-by-side with fully clothed princes, driving the Romans before them in strobe lighting. This was the most that could be done in this cramped space to suggest a battle, and the lack of theatrical spectacle meant that the whole sequence from V.i. to V.v. seemed a rather inflexible series of soliloquies for Posthumus. Here, intimate staging nega-tively made the point that this sequence depends upon a combina-tion of theatrical and verbal virtuosity; Nicholas Farrell's verbal skills were not enough in themselves.

In addition, the director's handling was less adroit here than elsewhere, and he made two major miscalculations. Following a suggestion cited in the new Arden edition (p. 162), the jailer was doubled with Cloten, and the results demonstrated the folly of the procedure. Bruce Alexander made every point as the jailer, and with a spontaneity lacking in his Cloten. Even so, the double meant that we inevitably kept thinking of Cloten while watching the jailer, and there are no useful connections to be made between these two characters. Much more unfortunate, however, was the appearance, or non-appearance, of Jupiter. Posthumus's father and mother emerged from the shadows, spoke clearly but with no suggestion that they were ghosts, and looked upwards – but virtually nothing happened. There was a roaring sound and then Jupiter's lines were delivered over the amplification system while the white shape of a tiny eagle was projected on to the stage floor, visible only to those sitting in the upper level of the audience. It was a total anti-climax. And what was so curious about it was that even in this restricted space, Jupiter could easily have appeared in much the same way as he did at Stratford, Ontario, and arguably at the Globe and Blackfriars. For at the back of the Other Place acting area there is a narrow upper level, supported by a pole, beneath with Posthumus slept. It is practicable, and has been used effectively for entrances 'above' in other productions. What is more, as I explained at the beginning of this chapter, there were dark diagonal lines, possibly suggesting eagle's wings, on the back wall, with the apex just above that upper level. All that was needed to give the impression of a god atop this 'eagle' would have been for Jupiter to step on to the upper level at that point. But the exact mechanics are unimportant. What matters is that a major physical manifestation is needed to crown this sequence. A fluttering projection and booming voice-over were insufficient to convey a sense of the numinous, just as a painted gauze and voice-over had been in Peter Hall's Stratford production thirty years before.

The final scene naturally worked best where it could build upon performances that had been strongly established earlier on. The play's upward arc was greatly assisted, for example, by the lovely smile of relief which illuminated Pisanio's face when he realised that Innogen was alive:

> It is my mistress.
> Since she is living, let the time run on
> To good or bad. (V.vi.128-30)

Such lines seldom make any impression, but here they were the natural response of a man who had to cope with difficult situations and who was not certain if he had taken the right decisions. His cheerful realisation that he had was heartening to see. It emphasised the unexpected benefits than can emerge from a production which assumes that story-telling and characterisation are worth taking seriously.

But it was Donald Sumpter's Giacomo who made the real discoveries in this scene, and he did so by employing once again the quiet, thoughtful, unhurried manner that he had used in the earlier scenes, and by developing the characterisation that he had begun there. He made the other characters wait while he slowly re-lived those earlier experiences – and in the process made us realise that his version of the events differs significantly from what we are actually shown in I.iv and II.iv. I have often wondered why Shakespeare gave Giacomo such an extensive recapitulation of those events, and since the speeches are usually either severely cut or pointlessly gabbled (as in the BBC television version), there had been few opportunities to discover why. Donald Sumpter at last made it clear. Throughout the speech, Giacomo presents a view of Posthumus's behaviour considerably more positive than what we have seen taking place, especially in this production. But in no adequate performance can the Posthumus of the wager scene appear 'too good to be / Where ill men were' (V.vi.159-60), because the lines will not permit such an interpretation. He is not 'as calm as virtue' (V.vi.175), but rash and provocative.

What we are hearing, in short, is Giacomo's *repentant* view of events, making light of Posthumus's responsibility for them, in order to intensify his own guilt, especially in relation to Innogen. 'Your daughter's chastity' (V.v.180) was here spoken especially slowly, not to savour his intrigue, as in the television version, but to pay tribute to its power. Sumpter cultivated pauses within lines to emphasise his own guilt and her purity; she taught him the difference ' 'Twixt amorous (*pause*) and villainous'. Similarly, in the next line, he stressed that he was 'quenched / Of hope (*pause*), not longing': the line honestly admitted a sexual desire which he now regretted (V.vi.196-7). And this narration, with its reinterpretation of events which the audience has already seen, also shed light upon the real problem with Posthumus's account of the battle: that recapitulates events *without* reinterpreting them.

Giacomo's confession, with its whitewashing of Posthumus, was then effectively contrasted with the man himself, not the idealised version of him, in his ensuing outburst. He may be repentant, but he expresses this repentance in the same extreme manner with which he earlier expressed his confidence and his disillusion – and it is the old Posthumus who strikes Innogen down. This moment, too, was given its full value, on her part as well as his. The Innogen who hurled herself at her husband and the Posthumus who struck her down were the same people who had embraced so passionately at the start. They had been chastened, but not altered, by their traumatic experiences; Giacomo was the only character who had changed. It was to Posthumus that Innogen said, very tenderly, 'That headless man / I thought had been my lord' (V.vi.301-2), as she clung to him, in this way exorcising the memory of that other body which she had passionately embraced earlier. She once again gave the impression of a great weight being lifted from her shoulders, this time permanently. For once, the focus of this scene was firmly upon Innogen, Posthumus, and Giacomo; for the first time in my experience, Belarius's blessing of the princes was quite unmoving, because no relationship had been established between them earlier on.

It is often remarked, with some justice, that repentance and forgiveness are not so overwhelming here as in Shakespeare's other late plays, that these qualities get lost in a labyrinthine scene too concerned with displaying its ingenuity in providing a multiple denouement, and even with mocking the action by insisting on its play-like nature. In this production, Giacomo's repentance and his forgiveness by Innogen as well as Posthumus stood out from the rest of the action and did seem overwhelming in its very sober quietness. Its understated conviction was worth any amount of knowing mockery of 'theatrical self-consciousness'. And yet the conviction coexisted with much laughter in this scene. It occurred at all the points specified by John Russell Brown in his article on laughter in the last plays:

> Cymbeline's 'Does the world go round?', the Doctor's 'I left out one thing [which the Queen confessed]', Belarius' 'My boys, there was our error' . . . and the sudden reappearance of the Doctor for the ludicrously neat 'by the Queen's dram she swallowed'. At these and other points the contrivance of the play's conclusion can appear hilariously complicated. (In J. R. Brown and Bernard Harris, eds., *Later Shakespeare*, 1966, p. 122)

These phrases can draw laughter primarily because they appear so pat on their cue. Brown adds that such laughter should be exploited and encouraged, partly so that 'moments of feeling . . . are all the sharper for contrast'. That was certainly the effect upon Giacomo's repentance, and such a contrast is of course a basic principle of Shakespeare's technique in an earlier comedy like *Twelfth Night*, where his control over these contrasts is very secure. It is perhaps less so in *Cymbeline*, where there is a problem in releasing too much laughter too soon. Instead of providing a sophisticated perspective on the action, it can seem simply to trivialise it, to suggest that the play is not really about anything. The stratagem of the Other Place production on this point was clear. Laughter was strictly controlled until the final scene when it could be allowed with safety because by then the emotional tensions and realities had been so securely established, and the audience, like the characters, could be allowed to release a tension that had been pent up for over three hours.

This raises a more fundamental question about the play. If this very convincing realisation of at least the 'main' plot saw no reason to play the scenes for laughs, it is possible that laughter is not so inherent in the situations as some critics assume. Take the central scene, Innogen by Cloten's corpse. About the trickiest lines, 'O Posthumus, alas, / Where is thy head? Where's that? Ay me, where's that?' (IV.ii.322-3), Brown says that 'the apparent reality as expressed here is so absurd that very few actresses have dared to use all the words provided' (p. 121). This production, like most others recently, did use them all, and the moment seemed far from absurd, as Brown acknowledges that it can: 'The whole soliloquy so mixes abrupt comedy with deepest feeling that, temporarily, the comedy is entirely subdued, becoming part of the terror of Innogen's nightmare-dream.' But the Other Place staging was so successful in its intense seriousness, drawing the audience into Innogen's situation, as to suggest that this is not a scene for laughs at all. It even caused me to wonder in retrospect whether T. C. Worsley's sympathetic movement between laughter and tears while watching Vanessa Redgrave's Innogen, smiling at her excess but persuaded by her grief, in fact conceded too much to laughter.

The Other Place production suggested that Shakespeare uses the theatricality to focus on the emotional situations and to make them as real as possible so that, for example, we believe that Innogen is dead and given ritual burial while it is happening, and then share in her grief over the body. Having experienced these moments fully, we can, in the final scene, but only then, be allowed the release from tension that laughter provides in realising (or remembering) that Innogen was drugged, not poisoned, and that 'that headless man [Innogen] thought had been [her] lord' was in fact Cloten wearing his clothes. We consciously register these things, in fact, as the characters' themselves do. The response to Bill Alexander's production demonstrated that, when interpreted intelligently and sensitively, the theatricality of this play urges the audience to share in, not remain aloof from, the narrative and the characters' experiences. Audiences still seem to find these basic theatrical qualities interesting and absorbing, which is why *Cymbeline* works so well in performance.

AFTERWORD

'An actors' play':
Peter Hall's second production,
National Theatre, 1988

In the spring of 1988, the RSC *Cymbeline* described in the previous chapter transferred from The Other Place in Stratford to The Pit, the studio theatre at the Barbican, the RSC's London home. At the same time, a second production of the play opened at the National Theatre's Cottesloe auditorium, together with *The Winter's Tale* and *The Tempest*, to make up a special season of late Shakespeare plays. All three were staged by the same director (Peter Hall) and designer (Alison Chitty), and played by the same group of actors. It must be unprecedented for two major productions of this play to be available to audiences at the same time. The public, clearly feeling a justifiable sense of deprivation, seized their opportunity, and both productions were sold out throughout their runs: many people commented that it made a pleasant change to see the play at all, let alone in two such notable stagings. A full account, not only of Peter Hall's production but also of the rehearsal process that preceded it, will appear in my book *Staging Shakespeare's Late Plays*, forthcoming from Oxford University Press; but it seemed appropriate to end with a brief account of it here, since it significantly modified and developed Hall's approach in his Stratford version of thirty years earlier, described in chapter II, and since there was general agreement that it made a strong case for the theatrical effectiveness of the play.

Although The Pit and the Cottesloe are both small theatres, these two productions could hardly have been more different, apart from a basic determination to take the play seriously and to do it justice in a very full text. Whereas the Pit/Other Place version showed the advantages and limitations of a studio approach, there was nothing small-scale about the Cottesloe production, which subsequently transferred to the National's large Olivier auditorium. The Cottesloe is roughly the same size as the Blackfriars, where early performances of the three late plays probably took place, so it seemed to Peter Hall an ideal space in which to begin an exploration of the plays. There was no attempt at a historical reconstruction of those early performances, but rather an investigation of three different aspects of a single imaginative world.

That world, in Alison Chitty's design, was a boldly simple, emblematic universe, firmly rooted in the seventeenth century. Above the stage hung a huge circular representation of the Copernican heavens with brilliantly gilded rays emanating from a golden sun, and surrounded by plants and signs of the Zodiac. Lamps were fitted into this circle, and when the moment came for the intervention of Jupiter, the heavens lit up, split apart and tilted, so that a gilded classical Jupiter could fly through them, seated on his golden eagle, exactly as the text implies; when he flew back to the heavens, the ceiling closed behind him, as he 'entered / His radiant roof' (V.v.214-15). At the back of the sloping stage floor was a wall painted with a *trompe l'oeil* image of sky and clouds based on masque designs of the period. Panels within this wall slid aside to provide entries, and there was a central doorway for all three plays, though presenting a different image for each. In *Cymbeline*, the door was of plain wood surrounded by a heavy stone-work frame hinting at the play's ancient British world.

The floor contained a circular central section, mirroring the circular heavens above it. For Britain and Rome it consisted of floorboards, but when the action shifted to Wales, the circular central section rose up from the front of the stage and flipped right over to reveal a new surface of rocks and grass. But just as the audience thought that the change had been completed, the moving section continued to descend, making the further revelation that beneath the back area of the stage was a cliff-face with fissured rocks and clumps of grass, the mountainous terrain of Wales; and within the cliff was the mouth of a cave. As the floor continued its descent, creating a steep slope from the centre of the stage down to the back of it, Basil Henson's genial Belarius appeared at the cave-mouth and clambered up the slope to the central point of the stage; as the whole stage was brilliantly illuminated by the early morning sun, he savoured the fresh air and exclaimed with smiling satisfaction, 'A *goodly* day!' (III.iii.1). This breathtaking *coup de théâtre* was absolutely in keeping with the overtly theatrical spirit of the play; and it perfectly established a complete change of locale, to healthy country air, to a place where Belarius and subsequently Innogen could be themselves, far from a restrictive court where people are expected to 'wear their faces to the bent / Of the King's looks' (I.i.13-14).

The basic costume style was that of 1640, Caroline rather than Jacobean: the men wore broad-brimmed plumed hats, lace collars and bucket-top boots, the women ringlets, silks, and brocades. Innogen first appeared as a radiant Caroline princess, a young Henrietta Maria from a Van Dyck painting; for her boy's disguise, she changed into a smart, comfortable suede page-boy's suit and boots. She wore her hair up in the court, and was simply able to let it down for her boy's disguise, since shoulder-length hair was the male fashion in 1640. But while the basic period was Caroline, other touches maintained the eclectic range of the play. While the Queen's dress, for example, was seventeenth-century in style, it also had medieval hanging sleeves; and Cymbeline wore a ground-length robe and a simple medieval crown. The Romans wore classical helmets and breastplates over their Caroline doublets. The apparitions of Posthumus's family were masked, classical figures from a remote antiquity. This was a subtler, simpler, and altogether more successful way of reflecting the play's eclecticism than the violent clash of periods in Hall's 1957 production.

Hall felt that his earlier version had caught the play's romance aspects but not its political ones. Here, he was keen to bring out the political content of all three plays, and one advantage of the 1640 designs was that they conjured up for a modern audience images of Charles I and therefore of political absolutism. In *The Winter's Tale*, Leontes is not just a jealous man, but 'a jealous *tyrant*': he can do so much harm because he is an absolute monarch. In *The Tempest*, the power struggles over the dukedom of Milan are central: Prospero is a prince as well as a magician, and the political tensions between himself and his brother remain unresolved at the play's ambiguous close. In *Cymbeline*, the destiny of Innogen is closely entwined with that of Britain: the crisis of the Innogen/Posthumus relationship on the personal level is reflected on the public one by the war between Britain and Rome, and the private reunion of husband and wife leads in turn to the public reconciliation of Britain and Rome.

This political framework enabled Tony Church to make much more of Cymbeline than the figure-head of most productions. He was a man torn apart, subject to ungovernable Lear-like rages, but also aware of true values beneath those rages. He had one superb moment of instinctive perception: as he waved farewell to Caius Lucius in III.v., and wished him 'Happiness! (III.v.17), all life seemed to drain from his face. It was as if he saw before him the horrors of war that his inflexibility, and the Queen's influence, were about to unleash upon Britain; but more than that was his intuition, perceived in a flash, that his public crisis was inextricably entwined with a private one. Moments later, Cymbeline asks 'Where is our daughter?' (III.v.30), and on being told that there is no answer from her rooms, fears the worst: 'Grant heavens that which I / Fear prove false' (III.v.52-3). What he fears presumably is that she is dead; Tony Church made it absolutely clear that Britain's danger was Innogen's too.

But for all the impact of its public frame, the heart of the production was the triangular relationship between Innogen, Posthumus, and Giacomo, and in particular the stern purgative processes that Innogen and Posthumus endure before their reunion. I have never known these so uncompromisingly presented. A basic assumption of this production was that both Posthumus and Innogen are rash and immature; both have to grow and to develop, and here they did so in extremely tough and harsh circumstances. Peter Woodward's Posthumus was at once rash and complacent: lines like 'She holds her virtue still, and I my mind' (I.iv.63) had something almost prim about them, which made him easy prey for a mocking hedonistic society in Italy, and especially for Tim Pigott-Smith's Giacomo. Like other recent performances of the role, this Giacomo was at once a part of this cynical society and yet set apart from it. On the one hand, the wager was provoked by Posthumus's complacency, a point vividly made by Pigott-Smith's mimicry of Woodward's priggishness at 'I make my wager ... against *your confidence*' (I.iv.108-9); but when Giacomo said 'If you buy ladies' flesh at a million a dram, you cannot preserve it from *tainting*' (I.iv.132-4), he turned sourly away from the company, packing a world of distaste and disillusion into the word 'tainting'.

This man, whose disillusioning experiences with women in the past had clearly made him cynical about all women, was then brought face to face with a woman who forced him to reconsider his values. This made for additional, fascinating tension in the bedroom scene. Innogen was evidently naked beneath the sheets, and Giacomo was overcome with desire. At the same time, Tim Pigott-Smith restored the balance of the scene which other recent Giacomos, especially Colm Feore's at Stratford, Ontario, have been in some danger of losing by throwing so much emphasis upon the near-rape and soiling of Innogen. Like Feore, Pigott-Smith kissed the mole on Innogen's breast – and since this Innogen was naked, the inflammatory nature of the gesture was greatly heightened. It intensified the temptation to take her by force, and so made all the more effective this Giacomo's refusal to do so; he was overwhelmed not only by her personal radiance but by her integrity and worth, which he could not bring himself to desecrate.

In this production, Innogen's scene with Pisanio in Wales emerged as her central crisis. This long and difficult scene is often heavily cut; but, playing the full text, Geraldine James was able to demonstrate the entire range of the role as she moved from one emotional extreme to another with exceptional virtuosity. After reading Posthumus's letter, she stood rooted to the spot in shock, the paper fluttering from her nerveless hands (an exact and effective parallel to Posthumus's dropping *her* letter at II.iv.105). The aching simplicity of 'False to his bed?' gave way to fury against the 'jay of Italy', and she effortlessly absorbed the tricky reference (usually cut) to the treachery of Aeneas and Sinon in a rising curve of passion, thereby demonstrating what the allusions are there for: Innogen expresses her disillusionment with Posthumus by generalising about male treachery, just as he earlier expresses his sense of betrayal by generalising about female infidelity.

There was nothing sentimental about her plea to Pisanio to kill her; and her tart reply when he said that he thought she 'would not back again' to the court, 'Most like, / Bringing me here to kill me' (III.iv.116-17) drew a sympathetic laughter from the audience which sharpened by contrast the moving sense both of her spiritual desolation and of her realistic acceptance of the situation in the simple phrase 'Dead to my husband' (III.iv.131). This performance made it clear that the extreme range of moods in the scene dramatise a character who is experiencing the most severe emotional crisis of her life so far, but who is also using impatience, indignation, even mockery as a means of releasing her feelings so as to gain control over them. Her recovery was naturally slow, but it was also sure, and it was clinched by the resolute, weighted delivery of the lines in which Innogen expresses her new resolution:

> I' th' world's volume
> Our Britain seems as of it but not in't,
> In a great pool a swan's nest. Prithee, think
> There's livers out of Britain. (III.iv.138-41)

But these lines also took on a wider implication in a production which made so much of the political context. Innogen, whose destiny is associated with Britain's, here looked beyond narrow patriotism and had a fleeting vision of the international peace and unity which concludes the play. That was one of the many things that emerged from a rich scene which takes the heroine on a journey from despair to new life.

In that respect, it anticipates the still more extraordinary emotional journey travelled by Innogen in the scene beside Cloten's corpse. And again Geraldine James was careful to chart the fluctuations of emotion. Like William Gaskill in 1962, Peter Hall did not compromise on the body: the full horror of the bloody, severed neck was fully revealed to the audience – but not, at first, to Innogen. The princes and Belarius had, as it were, reinstated Cloten's head by placing a huge cluster of flowers beside the neck, so when Innogen first awoke what she originally saw was a bloodstained corpse covered with flowers; it was not immediately evident that it was headless. She turned away in a half-waking, half-sleeping state – 'I hope I dream' – trying to shut out the fearsome object, but still aware that it was beside her, and finally forced to recognise that it was 'not imagined' but 'felt' (IV.ii. 309). Only then did she tentatively, gradually part the flowers and discover the truth, exactly where the text first mentions the fact: 'A headless man' (IV.ii.310).

That hideous realisation was instantly followed by a second: 'The garments of Posthumus'. She leapt to the erroneous conclusion in a flash, and both the shock and the certainty were so great that she only half-glanced at the various parts of the body as she alluded to them, which made much better sense than a very positive identification (as, for instance, in the BBC television version). Describing Peggy Ashcroft's performance in Hall's previous production, I suggested that the only way to play the last section of the speech is to pull all the stops out, because that is always how

I have seen it played. But Geraldine James's interpretation made me reconsider the point. She did indeed deliver 'O Posthumus, alas, / Where is thy head? Where's that? Ay me, where's that?' in a flood of passion, but she instantly pulled back on the next line, which was very tender and filled with heartfelt sadness:

> Pisanio might have killed thee *at the heart*
> And left thy head on. (IV.ii.322-3)

The pathos of this moment was typical of the way in which she skilfully graded the speech. And in the final lines, she lifted the body into her arms, embraced it, and buried her face in the bloody neck – as if substituting her own head for his – and in this way gave 'colour to [her] pale cheek with [his] blood' (IV.ii.332). There was another fine moment at the end of the scene: as the body she takes to be her husband's was carried ceremoniously from the stage, the light fell upon her drained, bloodstained face gazing steadfastly after it; there was a strong sense, as Elijah Moshinsky puts it, of the whole experience being 'a kind of therapy for her'.

Posthumus expiated his lack of faith in his wife in the still harsher environment of the war between Britain and Rome. He presented a nightmare image, his body caked with grime and streaming with blood, the 'bloody cloth' that Pisanio sent him wrapped around his head: his appearance was a vivid externalisation of the internal hell that he was enduring. The visual similarity between him and his bloodstained wife underlined that they go through similar ordeals. Both are brought to the point of despair and suicide, but while Innogen resists this temptation and rises above it, Posthumus gives way to it, seeking death on the battlefield. This Posthumus refused to believe Jupiter's promise of happiness and remained fatalistic in the episode with the jailer. Hall developed the technique he had used for the apparitions in 1957: they spoke the 'fourteeners' very rapidly and bewilderingly, a nightmare vision during which Posthumus writhed in agony on the floor, especially at the mention of Innogen.

His fatalistic mood persevered into the last scene, and was given a final twist at Innogen's 'Peace, my lord. Hear, hear': he actually recognised her voice, but refused to believe that she could be alive, and brutally struck her down. The moment was crueller than ever, but also absolutely true in psychological terms. This Posthumus was a man who lacked faith – in his wife at the start, in himself and the gods at the end. Seeing *Cymbeline* in close proximity to

The Winter's Tale made it clear that it could be said to Posthumus as appropriately as to Leontes, 'It is required / You do awake your faith' (*The Winter's Tale*, V.iii.94-5). It is not until the very end that he begins to do this – but the sight of this Posthumus and Innogen, grimy and bloodstained, finally achieving that embrace and clinging to each other amid the multiple revelations, was an image of happiness won through the harshest circumstances.

This sense of hard-won reconciliation was typical of Hall's approach to the play and of his handling of the final scene, from which almost all potential laughter had been banished. The series of revelations was taken absolutely seriously by a Cymbeline who was slowly coming to his senses, and it led ultimately to a very measured, weighty tableau of peace between Britain and Rome. It was at the furthest possible remove from the treatment of the finale in the RSC production at The Other Place, where the tensions pent up in both cast and audience for three hours were finally released in laughter. I am sure that both these stagings, in avoiding trivialising the characters and events, were absolutely true to the play, but I was not wholly convinced by Hall's ruthless excision of laughter from the final scene. It seems to me that Shakespeare does finally release laughter – not destructive or derisory laughter at the expense of the play or the characters, but a delight at the joy of reunion and reconciliation. Although audiences at the National were engrossed for most of the finale, the laughs that Hall had striven to avoid nevertheless broke out – rather uneasily – at some points for the simple reason that Shakespeare has written them in. Cornelius's 'I left out one thing which the Queen confessed' (V.vi.245) and Guiderius's 'I cut off's head, / And am right glad he is not standing here / To tell this tale of mine' (V.vi.297-9) are surely there to release unembarrassed laughter, and to intensify the pathos by contrast. This production could have afforded to relax rather more in the finale without at all endangering the sense of hard-won reunion.

But otherwise Hall caught all the qualities of the play as he did not in 1957: its theatricality, its eclecticism, its variety, its humanity, above all the sense of two people undergoing traumatic purgations. This trilogy of late Shakespeare drew a very warm response from both press and public, and it was widely considered that *Cymbeline* came off best of the three, a further testimony to its power in performance. In his review of the three plays in *The Times Literary Supplement*, Stephen Wall spoke for many reviewers when he said that *Cymbeline* 'seems to get more stage-worthy each time is done', and he even claimed that, when seen in the context of *The Winter's Tale* and *The Tempest*, '*Cymbeline* hangs together better than the other plays, despite its heterogeneous materials' (*TLS*, 10-16 June 1988). The reason is not far to seek: as Hall himself put it during rehearsals, this is basically 'an actors' play, for acting', and its full potential can only be fully realised in performance.

BIBLIOGRAPHY

Armstrong, E. A., *Shakespeare's Imagination*, London, 1946.

BBC TV Shakespeare, *Cymbeline*, London, 1983.

Brockbank, J. P., 'History and Histrionics in *Cymbeline*', *Shakespeare Survey 11*, 1958, 42-8, reprinted in *Shakespeare's Later Comedies*, ed., D. J. Palmer, Harmondsworth, 1971, 234-47.

Brown, Ivor, *Shakespeare Memorial Theatre 1957-9*, London, 1959.

Brown, Ivor, and Quayle, Anthony, *Shakespeare Memorial Theatre 1948-50*, London, 1951.

Brown, John Russell, 'Acting Shakespeare Today', *Shakespeare Survey 16*, 1963, 143-51.

—— 'Laughter in the Last Plays', in *Later Shakespeare*, ed. J. R. Brown and B. A. Harris, London, 1966, 103-25.

Bullough, Geoffrey, *Narrative and Dramatic Sources of Shakespeare*, VIII, London, 1975.

Byrne, Muriel St Clare, 'The Shakespeare Season', *Shakespeare Quarterly*, VIII, 1957, 461-92.

Clarke, Mary, *Shakespeare at the Old Vic*, London, 1957.

David, Richard, *Shakespeare in the Theatre*, Cambridge, 1978.

Dowden, Edward, ed., *Cymbeline* (Arden Shakespeare), London, 1903.

Edwards, Phillip, 'Shakespeare's Romances: 1900-57', *Shakespeare Survey 11*, 1958, 1-18.

Foakes, R. A., *Shakespeare: The Dark Comedies to the Late Plays*, London, 1971.

Gaines, Robert A., *John Neville Takes Command*, Stratford, Ontario, 1987.

Granville-Barker, Harley, *Prefaces to Shakespeare: Cymbeline*, London, 1930, reprinted 1984.

Harris, Bernard, '"What's past is prologue": *Cymbeline* and *Henry VIII*' in

Later Shakespeare, ed. J. R. Brown and B. Harris, London, 1966, 203-33.

Jones, Emrys, 'Stuart *Cymbeline*', *Essays in Criticism*, XI, 1961, 84-99, reprinted in *Shakespeare's Later Comedies*, ed. D. J. Palmer, Harmondsworth, 1971, 248-63.

Kemp, T. C., and Trewin, J. C., *The Stratford Festival*, Birmingham, 1953.

Kermode, Frank, *Shakespeare: The Final Plays*, London, 1963.

—— '*Cymbeline* at Stratford', *TLS*, 5 July 1974, p. 710.

Arthur C. Kirsch, '*Cymbeline* and Coterie Dramaturgy', *ELH*, 34, 1967, 285-306, reprinted in *Shakespeare's Later Comedies*, ed. D. J. Palmer, Harmondsworth, 1971, 264-87.

Knight, G. Wilson, *The Crown of Life*, Oxford, 1947.

Leech, Clifford, 'Shakespeare's Songs and the Double Response' in *The Triple Bond*, ed. J. G. Price, University Park, Pa., 1975, 73-91.

Lomax, Marion, *Stage Images and Traditions: Shakespeare to Ford*, Cambridge, 1987.

Maxwell, J. C., ed., *Cymbeline* (The New Shakespeare), Cambridge, 1960.

Nosworthy, J. M., ed., *Cymbeline* (new Arden Shakespeare), London, 1955.

Orgel, Stephen, ed., *The Tempest* (The Oxford Shakespeare), Oxford, 1987.

St John, Christopher, ed., *Ellen Terry and Bernard Shaw: a Correspondence*, London, 1931.

Schoenbaum, S., *William Shakespeare, a Documentary Life*, Oxford, 1975.

Schwartz, Murray M., 'Between Fantasy and Imagination: a Psychological Exploration of *Cymbeline*' in *Psychoanalysis and Literary Process*, ed. Frederick Crews, Cambridge, Mass., 1970, 219-83.

Shaw, G. B., *Our Theatres in the Nineties*, II, London, 1932.

Siemon, J. E., 'Noble Virtue in *Cymbeline*', *Shakespeare Survey 29*, 1976, 51-61.

Speaight, Robert, *Shakespeare on the Stage*, London, 1973.

Sutherland, James, 'The Language of the Last Plays' in *More Talking of Shakespeare*, ed. John Garrett, London, 1959, 144-58.

Tanitch, Robert, *Ashcroft*, London, 1987

Taylor, Michael, 'The Pastoral Reckoning in *Cymbeline*', *Shakespeare Survey 36*, 1983, 97-106.

Thomson, Peter, 'The Smallest Season', *Shakespeare Survey 28*, 1975, 137-48.

Tillyard, E. M. W., *Shakespeare's Last Plays*, London, 1938.

Trewin, J. C., *Shakespeare on the English Stage 1900-1964*, London, 1964.

Waith, Eugene M., 'The Metamorphosis of Violence in *Titus Andronicus*', *Shakespeare Survey 10*, 1957, 39-49.

Walker, Roy, 'Unto Caesar', *Shakespeare Survey 11*, 1958, 128-35.

Warren, Roger, 'Shakespeare at Stratford and the National Theatre, 1979', *Shakespeare Survey 33*, 1980, 169-80.

Wells, Stanley, 'Shakespeare and Romance' in *Later Shakespeare*, ed. J. R. Brown and B. A. Harris, London, 1966, 49-79.

Wells, Stanley, and Taylor, Gary, eds., *William Shakespeare: The Complete Works*, Oxford, 1986.

Wells, Stanley, and Taylor, Gary, *William Shakespeare: A Textual Companion*, Oxford, 1987.

APPENDIX

Principal casting
of major productions discussed

Stratford-upon-Avon, 1957

Director: Peter Hall   Designer: Lila de Nobili

Innogen	Peggy Ashcroft	*Queen*	Joan Miller
Giacomo	Geoffrey Keen	*Posthumus*	Richard Johnson
Cymbeline	Robert Harris	*Cloten*	Clive Revill
Pisanio	Mark Dignam	*Belarius*	Cyril Luckham
Arviragus	Brian Bedford	*Guiderius*	Robert Arnold

Stratford-upon-Avon, 1962

Director: William Gaskill   Designer: Rene Allio

Innogen	Vanessa Redgrave	*Queen*	Patience Collier
Giacomo	Eric Porter	*Posthumus*	Patrick Allen
Cymbeline	Tom Fleming	*Cloten*	Clive Swift
Pisanio	Tony Church	*Belarius*	Paul Hardwick
Arviragus	Barry MacGregor	*Guiderius*	Brian Murray
	Caius Lucius	Tony Steedman	

Stratford, Ontario, 1970

Director: Jean Gascon   Designer: Tanya Moiseiwitsch

Innogen	Maureen O'Brien	*Queen*	Pat Galloway
Giacomo	Leo Ciceri	*Posthumus*	Kenneth Welsh
Cymbeline	Powys Thomas	*Cloten*	Robin Gammell
Pisanio	Bernard Behrens	*Belarius*	Mervyn Blake
Arviragus	Stephen Markle	*Guiderius*	Leon Pownall

BBC Television (recorded 1982, shown 1983)

Director: Elijah Moshinsky   Designer: Barbara Gosnold

Innogen	Helen Mirren	*Queen*	Claire Bloom
Giacomo	Robert Lindsay	*Posthumus*	Michael Pennington
Cymbeline	Richard Johnson	*Cloten*	Paul Jesson
Pisanio	John Kane	*Belarius*	Michael Gough
Arviragus	David Creedon	*Guiderius*	Geoffrey Burridge

Jupiter   Michael Hordern

Stratford, Ontario, 1986

Director: Robin Phillips   Designer: Daphne Dare

Innogen	Martha Burns	*Queen*	Susan Wright
Giacomo	Colm Feore	*Posthumus*	Joseph Ziegler
Cymbeline	Eric Donkin	*Cloten*	Benedict Campbell
Pisanio	Nicholas Pennell	*Belarius*	Stephen Russell
Arviragus	Brent Stait	*Guiderius*	Keith Thomas

The Other Place, Stratford-upon-Avon, 1987, and The Pit, Barbican, London, 1988

Director: Bill Alexander   Costumes: Allan Watkins

Innogen	Harriet Walter	*Queen*	Julie Legrand
Giacomo	Donald Sumpter	*Posthumus*	Nicholas Farrell
Cymbeline	David Bradley	*Cloten*	Bruce Alexander
Pisanio	Jim Hooper	*Belarius*	Paul Webster
Arviragus	Paul Spence	*Guiderius*	David O'Hara

National Theatre, 1988

Director: Peter Hall   Designer: Alison Chitty

Innogen	Geraldine James	*Queen*	Eileen Atkins
Giacomo	Tim Pigott-Smith	*Posthumus*	Peter Woodward
Cymbeline	Tony Church	*Cloten*	Ken Stott
Pisanio	Tony Haygarth	*Belarius*	Basil Henson
Arviragus	Jeremy Flynn	*Guiderius*	Stephen Mackintosh

INDEX